1·00 M

A. E. Horton

The Story of
NEW SAN DIEGO
and of its Founder
ALONZO E. HORTON

SECOND EDITION, REVISED

By Elizabeth C. MacPhail

San Diego Historical Society

Library of Congress Catalog Card Number 79-63134
ISBN 0-918740-01-0

Published by the San Diego Historical Society
P.O. Box 81825
San Diego, California 92138

Printed by Crest Offset Printing Company
National City, California

Designed by Thomas L. Scharf

The cover illustration is a detail of "San Diego, December 28, 1891" by an artist named Hutchings and is from the art collection of the San Diego Historical Society. The front fly leaf is a "Bird's Eye View of San Diego, California, 1876" by E.S. Glover. An 1873 lithograph of San Diego by A.E. Mathews as "The Terminus of the Texas Pacific Railway" appears on the back fly leaf. Unless otherwise noted all photographs used throughout are from the San Diego Historical Society's Title Insurance and Trust Photograph Collection.

Contents

Illustrations

PREFACE

In San Diego's Horton Plaza there is a fountain that has been a familiar landmark since 1910. Embossed in the cement, with water cascading over them, are bas-relief portraits of three founders of San Diego. They are: Juan Rodríquez Cabrillo, discoverer of the harbor in 1542; Junípero Serra, Franciscan padre who established European civilization in Alta California on Presidio Hill in 1769; and Alonzo E. Horton, founder of the modern city of San Diego.

Since 1892, celebrations of some kind have been held each year in San Diego commemorating the landing of Cabrillo. For even longer, the anniversary of Father Serra's arrival has been noted, culminating in the city's 200th Anniversary celebration in 1969.

Little note was taken in 1967 of the 100th Anniversary of the founding of New San Diego by Alonzo E. Horton. Perhaps it is because, historically speaking, 100 years is a short time.

Only recently has the name of Horton been again in the news because of the city's Horton Plaza Redevelopment Project for the downtown area. Plans for a "Gaslamp Quarter" along Fifth Avenue from the waterfront to Broadway remind us that this is where Horton's town began in 1867. New interest has been taken and great progress is being made in restoring and preserving buildings from the Horton era.

Without in any way detracting from the importance and significance of the establishment of San Diego's first settlement at Old Town, we should recall the equally important story of the present city of San Diego, once called New Town, and of its founding by Alonzo E. Horton.

The purpose of this book is to introduce to San Diegans the man who was given the title "Father" not by any religious sect but by his fellow citizens who recognized him as the founder of their city. With the hoped for redevelopment of downtown San Diego it seems appropriate that San Diegans should be made aware that it was Alonzo E. Horton whose vision and enterprise first set in motion the city which is now called "America's Finest City."

Elizabeth C. MacPhail

San Diego, California
July, 1979

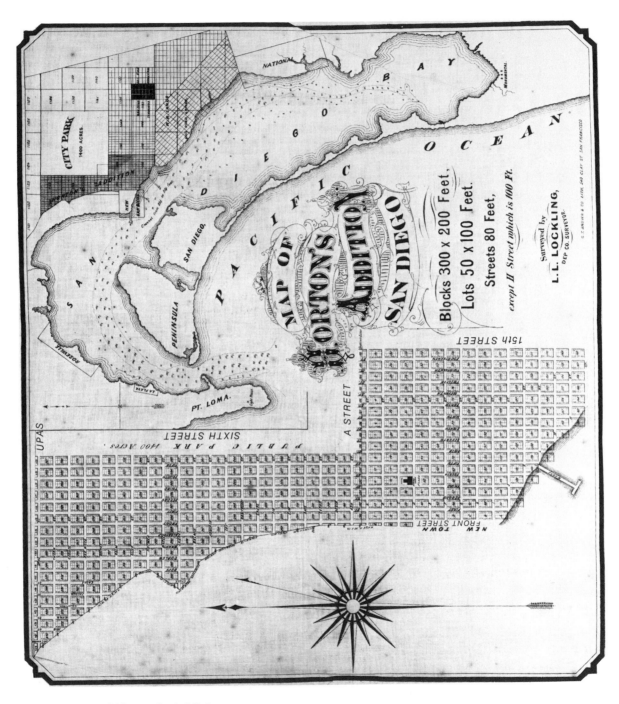

Fig. 1 Map of Horton's Addition

Chapter One

The Purchase, 1867

On April 15, 1867, the tiny steamer *Pacific* arrived from San Francisco with a handful of passengers for the Godforsaken village of San Diego. Most of the trading ships of that period landed at La Playa, but the *Pacific*, bringing six passengers and some freight, came up the bay to the foot of what is now Market Street. Here, seventeen years before, William Heath Davis had built a wharf but, by 1867, only a few piles marked its location. The bay was too shallow for ships to come close in, so passengers were taken by rowboat to the water's edge. Then, in order not to get their feet wet, they were carried to dry land on the backs of sailors or Indians.

One of the passengers on this trip was Alonzo E. Horton, a merchant from San Francisco. After being carried on the back of an Indian and deposited safely on dry land, he and the other passengers were told they would have to wait for a buckboard to come from the town three miles away to pick them up. While waiting, Horton walked up to a knoll, the site of the present courthouse, and looked over the lay of the land. It was a beautiful day and he could see clearly the outline of the bay, the peninsula (Coronado), Point Loma and the distant islands. Around him, as far as eye could see, was sagebrush. In the distance were a few Indian huts, but the only sign of life were the jack rabbits which scampered about.

What Horton saw, he liked. Later, in his own words, he said: "I thought San Diego must be a Heaven on Earth, if it was all as fine as that. It seemed to me the best spot for building a city I ever saw." So far as known, he is the first person to have used the expression "Heaven on Earth" in referring to this earthly paradise. Before that, most references to it had located it in the opposite direction.

When Horton got to what was then the site of San Diego (later to be called Old Town) he looked around a bit. It did not take long because all of the town could be seen while standing still. Someone then asked him what he thought of it. "I would not give you $5.00 for a deed to the whole of it—I would not take it as a gift. It doesn't lie right. Never in the world can you have a city here."

He was asked where he thought the city should be. "Right down there by the wharf. I have been nearly all over the United States and that is the prettiest place for a city I ever saw. Is there any land for sale?"

Before stopping to check in at what passed for a hotel, he was directed to George Pendleton, who bore the title of County Clerk, Clerk of the Court, and whatever other official title happened to be needed at the moment. Pendleton told Horton he could buy land by having it put up for sale at auction, but first, there would have to be a special election of trustees. There being no work for the trustees, the old ones had been holding over. Horton told Pendleton to go ahead and call an election.

Pendleton replied, "I shan't do it, sir. The town owes me enough already."

"How much would it cost to call an election?"

"Not less than five dollars."

Horton put his hand in his pocket, took out a $10 gold piece and said, "Here is ten dollars. Now call the election."

Horton himself helped Pendleton post the three notices that were required. Ten days' notice had to be given before the election could be held, so Horton lost no opportunity during that time to get acquainted with the residents who could give him information about the place he found so delightful. He struck up an acquaintance with Ephraim W. Morse, a merchant, and thus began a friendship which lasted all their lives. Morse had gone to San Francisco during the Gold Rush and later came to San Diego and opened a store. He became a partner with Thomas Whaley; founding the firm of

Fig. 2 Point Loma and San Diego
Bay much as Horton first
saw it

Fig. 3 An early view of San
Diego's Old Town

Whaley & Morse. When Horton arrived, Morse was not only in the mercantile business but served as an agent for Wells, Fargo & Company as well.

Morse accompanied Horton to show him land that was available, including that which would become known as "Horton's Addition." After a few days' stay, Horton discovered the cough that had plagued him for years had disappeared. He was told that was the way with everyone who came here, "They all get well right off, even if they have consumption."

When Sunday came, Horton attended services at the little Catholic chapel on Conde Street, it being the only church in town. When the plate was passed, he noticed only small coins, the most being ten cents. He had a $5.00 roll of silver coins that he put in the plate. This attracted considerable attention and after the services Father Ubach, the priest, went over to talk to this affluent stranger in town. He asked Horton if he were a Catholic. Horton told him no, he did not belong to any church. He then told Father Ubach why he was in town and about the coming election. Father Ubach asked him whom he wanted to be elected trustees. Horton said he would like E.W. Morse for one, but did not know the other businessmen very well. Father Ubach suggested that perhaps Joseph S. Mannasse and Thomas H. Bush would do for the other two. When the election was held on April 27 these three men were elected, each receiving thirty-two votes.

The auction was held on Friday, May 10. Sheriff James McCoy was the auctioneer. E.W. Morse acted as his deputy. The first tract put up for bid extended from where the courthouse is now located on Broadway, south to the waterfront, and east to Fifteenth Street. It contained about 200 acres. Horton's first bid was $100.00.

"The people around me began to laugh when they heard it. I thought they were laughing because I had bid so little, but on inquiring what it was customary to pay for land, I was told that $20 was a good price if the land was smooth, or about $15 if it was rough. I did not bid so much after that. I was the only bidder on all the parcels except one. On a fractional section near where Upas Street is now, Judge Hollister bid $5 over me. I told him he could have it, and then he begged me to bid again. I finally raised him 25¢ and then he would not bid any more."

Hollister said, "You can have it. I wouldn't give a mill an acre for all you have bought. That land has lain there for a million years, and nobody has built a city on it yet."

To which Horton replied: "Yes, and it would lie

Fig. 4 Ephraim W. Morse

there a million years longer without any city built on it, if it depended upon you to do it."

When the auction was over, Horton had purchased 960 acres for $265.00, or twenty-seven and a half cents an acre. The next day, Saturday, May 11, 1867 the Board of Trustees gave a deed to Horton which was recorded at 8:00 p.m. that day. On the same date, May 11, Horton registered as a voter in San Diego.

Horton returned on the next boat to San Francisco with the residents of Old Town satisfied that

Fig. 5   Joseph Mannasse

Fig. 6   George Pendleton and his wife.

Below:
Fig. 7   Father Antonio Ubach

he must have more money than brains. No man in his right mind would try to build a city on the spot, where seventeen years before, a prominent Californian, William Heath Davis had tried to establish a city and failed. They were justified in their skepticism because "Davis' Folly" was still fresh in their memory.

When Horton left, it was good riddance. He probably never would be heard from again. But they were mistaken, the City of San Diego had been born.

14

Chapter Two

Davis' Folly

In 1849, following the Mexican War, the Boundary Survey between the United States and Mexico was completed. One of the commission, camped at what is now the foot of Market Street, was Andrew B. Gray, a surveyor. He thought it was a perfect site for a city. In 1850 Gray was introduced to William Heath Davis, a San Francisco merchant and coast trader, who had married into the Estudillo family of San Diego. At that time he was a wealthy financier, living in San Francisco, but visiting occasionally in San Diego. Gray imbued Davis with his enthusiasm and the two formed a partnership, along with several other prominent residents, for the purpose of establishing the new town. In March they purchased from the City Trustees, for $2304, a tract consisting of 160 acres, bounded by what is now Front, Broadway and the waterfront. Davis, as a part of the deal, agreed to build a wharf. The wharf, located at approximately the foot of Market Street, was completed a few months later at a cost to Davis of $60,000. It was 600 feet long and L shaped. Later a government store and supply house was built at the end of the wharf. Military supplies were landed there and then carried by pack train to other parts of California and to Fort Yuma.

At that time, government troops, needed to defend the Indian and Mexican frontier, used the San Diego Mission as their headquarters. In 1850 a United States Government official was sent to San Diego to locate new barracks for the troops. It was expected the location selected would be at La Playa. However, Gray and Davis convinced the official that the barracks should be in "New Town" and offered the government a grant of land at what is now Market and Kettner, which was accepted. The government official, incidentally, became a partner in the New Town venture.

The residents of Old Town were sure the new town would fail. It was too far from water and wood. Davis solved the wood problem by bringing it in by boat from the north and east. But water was another matter. It had to be hauled from the river. Finally a few wells were drilled, giving Broadway its first name, Spring Street.

Fig. 8 William Heath Davis

16

The barracks were built from wood brought around the Horn. The building was two and a half stories in height, with a veranda on two sides, and a lookout and flagpole on top. A cistern was built, hopefully to catch rainwater. The troops used the block bounded by F, G, Union and State as a corral for their horses. This block was later donated to the federal government by the Davis group.

The partnership deeded to public use as a plaza the block bounded by Columbia, India, F and G. This became the center of town. A flag pole was erected, but it was not until 1887 that the block was landscaped.

Davis purchased a shipment of prefabricated houses from Portland, Maine, which came around the Horn on the brig *Cybele*. Soon there were a few houses, two hotels, a lumber yard and three stores. According to Davis the first house completed was one he built for himself, at the northeast corner of State and F Streets. Water for use in this house was carried from the well near Spring Street.

Fig. 11 The Barracks were built from wood brought around the Horn

The plaza and a hotel were named for Juan Pantoja, the Spanish navigator who mapped San Diego Bay in 1782. One hotel, Pantoja House, located on the east side of the plaza, had a saloon and billiard room and advertised "As good wines and liquor as can be procured on the Pacific Coast." Water was scarce, but there was no reason for anyone to be thirsty.

Another hotel was the Hermitage, on State between Market and "I" Streets, originally built as the home of Andrew B. Gray. It was over a store at G and Arctic (Kettner) that John Judson Ames, on May 29, 1851, first published a weekly newspaper called the *San Diego Herald*. It later gained fame, after moving to Old Town, when its part-time editor, Lt. George Horatio Derby, made it noteworthy and himself immortal by his humorous articles written under the pen name of John Phoenix.

Gray was not so successful in his attempt to get a post office at New Town. His efforts to obtain a customhouse also failed. Although New Town seemed to become the center of government activity, Old Town remained the County Seat.

In 1851 a fire in San Francisco cost Davis $700,000 and he felt he had to retrench. No more money would be forthcoming to bolster up the little town. By 1852 the struggle for supremacy was over—both New Town and La Playa gave up to Old Town.

There began a rapid exodus from the new town, not only of people but of the buildings. Most of the buildings were moved to Old Town. There was not enough business at the wharf to justify anyone collecting the fees. Although it was used now and

Fig. 9 William Heath Davis House, the oldest building still standing in New San Diego

Opposite:
Fig. 10 Andrew B. Gray

Fig. 12 Lt. George Horatio Derby

Above:
Fig. 13 Derby's sketch of John P.
Squibob

then, the wharf was allowed to disintegrate. In 1853 a steamer rammed it and the damage was never repaired.

The barracks continued to be used on and off and in 1858 became headquarters for the Southern Division of the U.S. Army of the Pacific. When the Civil War broke out most of the troops were transferred to the East, and many who were Southern sympathizers left to join the Army of the Confederacy.

During the winter of 1861-62 unusually heavy rains fell in San Diego county. The small number of troops at the barracks were marooned and ran out of fuel. The officer in charge decided, as a military necessity, to demolish what was left of the wharf and use it for firewood. Davis later presented a claim to the United States government. From 1862 until 1885 his claim was before Congress from time to time. At one time the Senate passed a bill for $60,000 reimbursement, but it failed to pass the House. Davis made many trips to Washington, at much cost and hardship. Finally, in 1885 Congress voted him $6,000 in full settlement of his claim.

In 1887, on a visit to San Diego, Davis was inter-viewed by a reporter from the *San Diego Sun*. In referring to his attempt to establish a city in New Town, he was quoted as saying "At that time I predicted that San Diego would become a great commercial seaport from its fine geographic position and from the fact that it was the only good harbor south of San Francisco. Had it not been for our Civil War, railroads would have reached here years before Stanford's road was built, and our wharf was ready for business."

In 1866 the barracks were vacated and the site of New Town was deserted of all human habitation, to become a haven for jack rabbits.

Since the wharf was destroyed, the few boats that came into the harbor landed their passengers on the sand spit adjacent to the old wharf, known as "Punta de los Muertos" or Point of the Dead. It had acquired its grizzly name when a Spanish fleet in 1782 had stopped to bury its dead in this sand spit before continuing on to land near Old Town. It was at this spot in 1867 that Alonzo E. Horton was first put ashore and thus began the second, and this time successful, attempt to establish a city in that location.

Chapter Three

The Man Horton

Who was this man who arrived at Old Town, unannounced and unknown, and who left a few weeks later owning what soon became, and still remains, the most valuable tract of land in the City and County of San Diego?

Not all of the facts concerning Horton's early life are known, but what is known establishes him as one of the bold and adventurous breed that developed the West in the mid 1800's. Had he also been ruthless and grasping he might have gained more fame and certainly more wealth. Ruthless and grasping he was not. He died a poor man, but with the love and respect of his fellow citizens. And with that, he was content.

Alonzo Erastus Horton was born October 24, 1813, in Union, Connecticut, one of seven children of Erastus Horton and Tryphena Burleigh Horton, both descended from old New England families. His brothers and sisters were Minerva, Emily, Ezra, Nelson, Thomas LaFayette and Lucy.

The family moved to New York state where Alonzo grew up. He was obliged to go to work while still very young to help support the family. He worked at many small odd jobs, was a clerk in a grocery store and then a sailor on the Great Lakes. His father was very strict, and although Alonzo often threatened to leave home, he stayed with his family until just before his twenty-first birthday when he paid his father $50 for the release of his minority. He acquired a small schooner and engaged in transporting grain between Oswego, New York, and Canada. For a short time he taught school in Oswego. At the age of twenty-one he was elected Constable on the Whig ticket in Oswego. However, Horton was not considered very successful because he was unable to put poor people out of their homes. He held the office only one term. About that time, he developed a cough and it was thought he might have consumption. He was advised to go West. This came as a great shock not only to Horton but to his family and friends. He was thought to have been in fine health and was known as a champion boxer.

"West" to Horton in 1836 was Milwaukee. His shrewd and resourceful business acumen showed up there, where he traded in land and cattle. His past record served him well. A story was told that when Alonzo was eight years old he sold a pig for $1.00. By mistake, the man gave him $2.00. The next day Horton returned the $1.00. By coin-

Fig. 14 Alonzo Horton as a young man

Fig. 15 Lucy Jane Horton

Foreleaf:
Fig. 16 Tryphena Horton

Fig. 17 Erastus Horton

cidence, the two met again years later in Wisconsin and the purchaser remembered the incident. He told a large group of citizens in Wisconsin, "I would trust Horton with everything I have in the world." His confidence was well placed. At times Horton's sanity may have been questioned but never his honesty or integrity. Early in life he stated his philosophy "My principle is to be as happy as I can every day; to try to make everyone else as happy as I can, and to try to make no one unhappy."

In 1841, at Jefferson, Wisconsin, Horton married Sally Millington Wright, who died of consumption in 1846. This is generally believed to be the first of three marriages. However, Horton's nieces, Grace Bowers and Vine Bowers Hill, have been quoted as saying their uncle was married five times. George

W. Marston, whose family knew Horton in Wisconsin, said Horton had married a Miss Trusser of Ft. Atkinson, Wisconsin, and that she was "a dressmaker and a very fine woman." If there were two other marriages, including the one to Miss Trusser, they were before 1860.

At the close of the Mexican War Horton went to St. Louis where he had heard land warrants could be purchased cheaply. With what money he could scrape up, he acquired 1500 acres, at seventy cents an acre, in Outagamie County, Wisconsin, and there founded his first city which was given the name Hortonville.

Hortonville is a small town situated about twenty miles from Oshkosh and a few miles north of Lake Winnebago. Perhaps, had Horton remained there, the "ville" would have been dropped and the city of Horton would have become an important metropolis.

A few years after founding Hortonville, Horton sold out his interests and with $7000 came to California for the first time. It was 1851 and the gold rush was on. He worked in the mines, was an Adams Express rider, traded in gold dust and then opened a store at Pilot Hill. Another interesting business he developed was trading in ice. He went into the mountains in El Dorado County and cut ice and brought it to the towns. He cut a total of 312 tons of ice, and from this venture made a profit of $8000. By 1854 he was a wealthy man by the standards of the time.

In 1857 he decided to return home, and took passage on the steamer *Cortez* for Panama. At that time, passengers for the East disembarked at Panama, crossed the Isthmus by land and took another ship on the other side for the rest of the journey. In Panama a riot broke out and natives began attacking foreigners. Horton and other passengers were dining in a hotel when the mob attacked. Horton was designated the leader for the defense of the passengers. They rushed to the upper story of the hotel. Horton stood at the head of the stairs, a revolver in each hand, cool and collected. As the attackers started up the stairs there was a shot and the leader fell dead. When two others took his place, they too were felled. Horton emptied his own weapons and all the others that were handed him, one by one. After eight of the attackers were killed and others wounded they moved back. With the revolvers distributed among the men the little group of passengers retreated to their ship, the mob following closely on their heels. All got on board safely. Most of the credit was given to Horton for his leadership and cool head.

Horton's baggage, containing $10,000 in gold dust, fell into the hands of the rioters. However, he still had $5,000 which was in a belt around his waist.

Horton spent several years in the East. On June 25, 1860, at Jersey City, he married Sarah Wilson Babe who shared his life, with its successes and failures, for the next thirty years. To him, she was always "Babe."

While in the East, Horton went to Washington, D.C., in an effort to settle claims for himself and others arising from the riot in Panama. He was successful in securing settlements for others, but for himself he got nothing. The government of New Granada (Colombia) refused to pay him anything because of his "front line" action which resulted in the deaths of several of its citizens and because of his representation of other claimants. His activities in Washington brought him to the attention of Secretary of State Seward who offered him a job in the State Department, but the lure of the West was too much. He returned to Wisconsin to visit his family, and then went to British Columbia where he located a claim in the Cariboo mining district. In 1862 he returned to San Francisco and opened a store at the corner of Sixth and Market Streets, where he sold furniture and household goods.

One night early in 1867 Horton attended a meeting at which the speaker described all the ports of the West Coast starting at Seattle and ending at San Diego. The speaker said San Diego was one of the healthiest places in the world and had one of the best harbors in the world. That was enough to start Horton thinking. He went home and got out a map of California and looked for San Diego. That night he slept little, turning his thoughts over and over until he was satisfied that this was the opportunity he had been waiting for. Could San Diego be the end of the rainbow for him? In the morning he told his wife he was going to sell his business and go to San Diego. She thought he must be out of his mind. Who ever heard of San Diego? By some stroke of luck, or fate, within three days he disposed of all his merchandise and had bought passage on the next steamer for San Diego.

Horton was then fifty-four years of age, beyond the prime of life for those times. He was of stocky build, five feet and ten inches in height, and presented a stately appearance. He was not loud or flamboyant, as might be expected, but reserved in manner. He was moderately well-off, but not wealthy, and far from being a millionaire. But he did have a practical vision and strength of

character, and he was a superb salesman in the very best sense of the word. He had that rare quality of being able to imbue others with his enthusiasm and confidence. The time and place were ripe for such a man. And for San Diego, he was the Man of the Hour.

Fig. 18 Alonzo and Sarah Wilson Babe Horton

Chapter Four

The "Paper" Town

As soon as Horton returned to San Francisco, after his land purchase in San Diego, he opened a land promotion office on Montgomery Street. To all who would listen he extolled the virtues of the site on which he was going to build a new city. He told of its beauty, its healthful climate and its fine harbor—the best south of San Francisco. Large crowds came asking for more information, in spite of the fact that many were aware that William Heath Davis, a prominent resident of San Francisco, had lost a fortune a few years earlier trying to do the same thing. Now, the times were different. Newcomers were arriving daily from the East, after having taken Greeley's advice to "Go West, Young Man." They were anxious to learn all they could about California and what lay south of San Francisco.

One of those who came to listen was General William S. Rosecrans. Rosecrans had resigned from the army after the Civil War and came to California as one of the incorporators of the Southern Pacific Railroad. He told Horton he would like to visit San Diego to see if a railroad could be built from San Diego eastward to Yuma. If it could, Horton's property would be worth millions. On Horton's next trip south Rosecrans accompanied him. They hired a team, and with several others went first to Tijuana, and then to Jacumba Pass where they could view the desert. General Rosecrans said "Horton, this is the best route for a railroad through the mountains I have ever seen in California."

As they returned through Horton's Addition, Rosecrans jokingly remarked that if he ever owned a lot in San Diego, "I would like it right here." Horton remembered this casual remark and the approximate location. After the land was surveyed and lots set out Horton made Rosecrans a present of the block bounded by Fifth, Sixth, F and G.

As a result of Rosecrans' visit, Horton was of-fered $100,000 for his property. When he was slow about accepting the offer, it was raised to $200,000 and then to $250,000. After thinking it over, Horton decided if it was worth that much to others, he might as well keep it, build the city himself, and keep the profit.

As soon as he could, Horton had a survey made of his purchase. It lay just east of Davis' New Town Addition and the tract known as Middletown. In May, 1850, soon after Davis had made his purchase, another group of prominent residents, including Oliver S. Witherby, Cave J. Couts, A. Haraszthy, J.M. Estudillo, Juan Bandini, and others, received a grant of 687 acres between New Town and Old Town and called it Middletown. No effort was made by those owners to develop it until after Horton arrived on the scene.

Horton's purchase consisted of Pueblo Lots. It was necessary to replat the area into city blocks and lots. On his trips to San Diego he could be seen plodding over his land, often in the company of E.W. Morse, with tape measure and stakes.

The boundaries of Horton's Addition can best be described by starting at the foot of Front Street, going north to Upas, east to Sixth, south to A, east to Fifteenth, and south to the waterfront. An additional wedge-shaped tract extends west on Upas to Jackdaw and then cuts back diagonally to Front at Cedar. As can be seen, this includes all of what is now the heart of the city.

Andrew B. Gray had platted New Town, laying out blocks and streets, and Horton followed Gray's plat. The streets starting at the bay from west to east were Ocean, Water, Atlantic (Pacific), California, Arctic (Kettner), India, Columbia, State, Union and Front. The next street, and the first in Horton's Addition, became First Street. The eastern boundary of Horton's Addition was Fifteenth Street. The streets starting at the bay from south to north, on Gray's map, were named Front, Pacific, Commercial, Fourth, Fifth and Sixth. Seventh Street became known as Spring Street (Broadway). Horton's map changed this. He started at the northernmost street which ran all the way from the waterfront east to Fifteenth and called it A Street. From A Street south to the waterfront, the streets went alphabetically. Front Street ended at J, but because of the curving of the bay, Fifteenth Street extended to "O" or the waterfront. From A Street north and west the streets were named alphabetically for trees and birds. House numbers began with 100 at the foot of Fifth Street in Horton's Addition, and this has not changed.

Numbering from west to east also began at the waterfront so that the block between Fourth and Fifth, now the 400 Block, was the 1300 Block. It was not until 1914 that the blocks were renumbered, starting at First Street. This is confusing to persons trying to locate an old address. One must remember to deduct 900 from the old address to arrive at the present block number. Also, it must be remembered that until about the same time, Market Street was H Street, and Broadway was D Street.

The map of Horton's Addition which is most familiar is the one made for Horton by L.L. Lockling, Deputy County Surveyor. This was the final survey, showing all the lots, blocks and streets in Horton's Addition. Each block was 200 x 300 and contained twelve lots, 50 x 100. No alleys were provided because Horton thought they were just a place for trash to collect. Because blocks were short, there were more of them, and consequently more corner lots, always more valuable. Streets were eighty feet wide, except for H (Market) which was 100 feet, and Horton later jogged D Street (Broadway) at Third,

making it 100 feet wide to the waterfront. This was to give his hotel, the Horton House, an unobstructed view down D Street to the waterfront.

Now, Horton had a map he could show prospective buyers. His city was laid out on paper, or on cloth. He had a number of maps printed in San Francisco on cloth. A few of these cloth maps still exist and are a rare collector's item. From this time on Horton was seldom seen without his map case, in the shape of a tin horn. He carried it wherever he went.

In San Francisco he would stop people on the street and point out on a rough map where his land lay and what his plans were for a new city. He would extol its beautiful location, its perfect harbor, the climate that was unsurpassed anywhere in the world, and, relying on Rosecrans' enthusiasm, assured his listeners that soon San Diego would become the southern railroad terminus from the East. Even on board ship, as he went back and forth between San Diego and San Francisco, he would buttonhole all who would listen. To most, however, his words fell on deaf ears. He became known as "that crazy man with a tin horn." Horton's San Diego was just a paper town, and that was all it ever would be.

Captain Phineas Banning, who operated a tugboat out of San Pedro, once gave fifty cents to an acquaintance who was going to San Diego, and said "Here, take this and buy Horton's Addition for me. You can keep the change."

Fig. 19 A mural depicting Horton selling his New Town lots

Courtesy J. Victor Guthrie

Chapter Five

Building a City From Scratch, 1868–69

When Horton arrived in San Diego the only buildings left standing in Davis' Addition were three dilapidated old houses, and the barracks which had become a pigeons' roost. Horton bought from Davis for $100 the house and lot at the northeast corner of State and F, which had been Davis' home. He sold it for $1000, sight unseen, to Captain Samuel Sumner Dunnells with the understanding it would be used as a hotel. If Dunnells was not satisfied with his purchase he could have his money back. Dunnells may have been discouraged when he saw the building for the first time, but the prospect of being the only hotel available for the many who would be coming to New San Diego made it look better, and in 1868 he opened Dunnells' Hotel, later known as the New San Diego Hotel. Now, Horton's prospective customers did not have to go to Old Town to find accommodations. By the end of 1868, the following advertisement for Dunnells' Hotel was appearing in the *San Diego Union*, a weekly newspaper which started publication in Old Town on October 10, 1868:

"This splendid new and First Class Hotel is now open. New furniture throughout. All persons visiting San Diego in search of health, recreation or pleasure will find good accommodations at this House. It is pleasantly situated near the steamer landing. The table is constantly supplied with the best the market affords and every attention is paid to the comfort and convenience of guests. Stages leave for all parts of California, Arizona and Mexico."

Reference to the steamer landing was to the new pier being built by S.S. Culverwell at the foot of F Street. Culverwell was trying to get ahead of Horton, who was also building a wharf in his Addition at the foot of Fifth Street. The first construction by Horton in his New Town was the wharf, completed in 1869 at a cost of $45,000. As a consequence, the town developed around the wharf and Fifth Street became the main street of the new town.

The first buildings in Horton's Addition were on free lots. Horton persuaded a group of skeptics to come down and look over his property. They were staying at Dunnells'. Horton offered each a free lot, not a corner one, on condition he would put up a house which would be at least twelve feet wide, sixteen feet long, and twelve feet high. As a result of this offer, twenty buildings went up on Fifth Street near the water front. This was the beginning of New San Diego. However, the only one of the original recipients who remained any length of time was Joseph Nash, who opened the first general merchandise store, at Fifth and J, on August 4, 1868. His letterhead carried the statement: "Established 1868. Pop. 23." The price on the first lots sold by Horton was $10.00.

Horton and his wife did not come to San Diego to live until November, 1868. He had been busy going back and forth between San Diego and San Francisco talking to prospective residents, and selling lots, which were starting to go like the proverbial hot cakes. The November 21, 1868, issue of the *San Diego Union* reported "At New Town buildings are in process of erection in all directions. We were told Mr. Horton is selling from $600 to $1000 worth of lots every day."

On November 7, Horton arrived on the *Orizaba* and said he had engaged the brig *S.B. Foster* to bring lumber for his wharf and that it would also bring Mrs. Horton, five other families, and all their furniture.

The Hortons first lived in one of the old Davis' houses, located on the northeast corner of Market and State Streets. This house was moved in 1873 to 227 Eleventh Street. Horton had reserved the block bounded by Ninth, Tenth, G and H for his residence. Soon after arriving in San Diego to live he started construction of his first home. He took pride in the fact that it would be the most "ornamental" house yet built in San Diego. This house, a one and a half story, and pretentious for

Fig. 20 W.W. Bowers

the times, became known as Cypress Cottage, and later as The Gables.

The first business building put up by Horton was a small frame one on Fifth between J and K. This became his first office. He next constructed a two-story building on Fifth between H (Market) and "I", and a two-story brick building on Sixth between J and K, which then became his office and later the first office of the Bank of San Diego.

Much of the payment for lumber, supplies and labor for his buildings and wharf was taken in lots, even whole blocks, which in many instances Horton later bought back when the owners became disenchanted and wanted to leave town. Some who received the lots were not even interested enough to record their deeds.

By January, 1869, Horton stopped selling blocks, only lots. He said the demand had become so great for lots that he would sell only to those who intended to improve the property and settle in San Diego. As a matter of fact, it would seem he was doing a favor letting people buy lots from him at any price. People were now arriving in such large numbers there was no accommodation for all of them. Many camped on their lots until buildings could be put up.

The next hotel, and the first in Horton's Addition, was The Bayview, opened in 1868 at Fifth and F. The proprietor was R.D. Case. By 1869 The Bayview was at Twelfth and "I" in a more pretentious two-story building. It was then advertising in the Union: "View from the Hotel is one of the finest in San Diego...The climate of San Diego is the most delightful and health giving on the Pacific slope. Persons seeking health and recreation can find no pleasanter place in the Golden State. This hotel is a fine 2 story house with large and well ventilated rooms. It is the only hotel in San Diego that is lathed and plastered—it is perfectly dry." This hotel was demolished and a new one built in 1889. That building still stands, known as The Palms.

The old barracks had been cleaned up and was used as a meeting hall. On Christmas Eve of 1868 all the residents of the new town gathered at the "town hall", the barracks, for a merry time. There was a beautifully decorated Christmas tree, gazed on with awe and admiration. Gifts were deposited under the tree. Joseph Nash gave each of the ladies material for a calico dress. At twenty cents a yard this was a very generous gift. Supper was enjoyed, perhaps the first "pot-luck" dinner in San Diego. Dancing followed into the wee hours of Christmas Day. It was an event long to be remembered by all those present.

The barracks was also used as a school until Horton donated lots and a small building at the northeast corner of Sixth and B for a school. Soon there were three little clapboard buildings on the lot which became known as the "little pink school" or "little yellow school" depending on the current shade of "whitewash."

Horton, although not a member of any organized church, realized that every city must have churches. To each religious denomination that started a church in San Diego he offered two free lots. The Baptists were the first to take advantage of his offer. The First Baptist Church was organized June 5, 1869, and started building on lots given it by Horton on Seventh near F. Their building was completed in October, 1869. Since it was the first church to be completed, and had a steeple, Horton donated the church bell, the first in San Diego. That church bell still tolls from the tower of the present church at Tenth and E. Horton's mother

Fig. 21   Dunnells' Hotel, later the
New San Diego Hotel, State
and F Streets

was a devout Baptist and attended services
regularly after her arrival in 1869 until her death in
1873. Horton was frequently seen slipping into
church on Sunday to sit beside her.

The Presbyterians organized the same month as
the Baptists with thirteen charter members. They
met in homes and later at Horton's Hall and then
built on lots given them by Horton at Eighth and D
(Broadway).

The Methodists met first in February, 1869, in
the barracks, and in 1870 built on their gift lots at
the northeast corner of Fourth and D.

The Episcopalians were the first to hold a
religious service in New San Diego. It was on
November 8, 1868, in the barracks. Reverend
Sidney Wilbur played a melodeon as well as
preached. The melodeon belonged to Captain
Dunnells. The press reported, "The service was
well attended and the congregational singing was
delightful." In 1869 a two story church building
was constructed on the lots donated by Horton on
the northeast corner of Sixth and C. Living
quarters for the minister were upstairs. Later that
building was removed and Trinity Hall built on the

site. The name of the church was The Parish of the
Holy Trinity. In 1871 Trinity Hall was moved to the
southeast corner of Fourth and C on lots given by
Horton in trade for the two lots at Sixth and C. In
1886 this site was sold for the Brewster Hotel and a
new church was built on the southwest corner of
Eighth and C and the name changed to St. Paul's.

During these early years Horton was the principal employer in San Diego. Many workmen were
recruited from San Francisco and elsewhere. One
requirement for employment by Horton was that
each man, besides being qualified at his trade,
must be a Republican, or at least agree to vote
Republican while in San Diego. Horton, even in
those early days of the Republican party, was a
"dyed in the wool" Republican. It must be
remembered he came from Wisconsin, the birth-
place of the Republican party. While in Old Town
in 1867 he let it be known he was a "Black"

Republican in contrast to southern sympathizers referred to as "Copperheads." Horton was warned that San Diego was a real Copperhead hole and he had better not talk politics there if he wanted to get back to San Francisco alive. He brazenly prophesied, "Then I will make it a Republican hole." In the general election of 1871 the city and county went Republican for the first time, and with only a few lapses since, has continued to be a "Republican hole."

In February, 1869, at the Franklin House in Old Town, Horton was nominated as a candidate for City Trustee. In his acceptance speech he said he was interested not only in New Town but also in Old Town, and would work for the welfare of both. At the election on March 1 he was defeated. This is understandable, not only because of his politics, but because the Old Towners were not happy about the emergence of New Town. There was jealousy and antagonism between the two towns, and the Old Towners, being a majority, were not about to elect to office the man who was responsible for New Town.

In March the wharf was nearing completion. It would be 2000 feet long and "T" shaped, with a warehouse at the end. Before completion of Horton's wharf most of the ships had been using Culverwell's wharf, but it did not extend far enough into deep water for all ships and when Horton's was completed the larger vessels came up the bay to the new wharf. Culverwell's, later Jorres', at the foot of F, was still used but mostly by smaller ships carrying freight.

On March 24 Horton sold $5500 worth of lots in the one day, and said it was not a record day. Now 124 houses had been completed, and Horton could look over his town with satisfaction. Frequently he would go up the hill, to First and Fir, and look over his city and watch its growth. He vowed that on this hill he would someday build another home for himself.

When a number of houses had been built up on the hill near where San Diego High School now stands, Horton told the owners if they would whitewash their houses he would furnish the brushes and lime. They did not act fast enough to suit him, so he hired men to whitewash one-half of the houses on the south and west sides, facing the bay, which could be seen from the steamers as they came in. Most of the owners finally finished the job themselves and the houses then made a fine show. People coming in on steamers thought the city was growing very fast, and were impressed.

In 1869 the town acquired its first doctor. He was Dr. Jacob Allen, whose office and residence was in a one-story building on the northeast corner of Fifth and F. He was also the druggist. In April, when South San Diego finally received its own post office, Allen became the postmaster with the Post Office being located in his drugstore. Soon Dr. Robert J. Gregg, who had established a practice in Old Town in 1868, moved over to New Town, on Fifth Street opposite Dr. Allen, just in case Dr. Allen was too busy being both druggist and postmaster to attend to all the patients. Dr. Gregg, it is said, walked most of the way to California from Peoria, Illinois. Dr. Allen after a few years moved to Riverside, but Dr. Gregg remained many years, a beloved and respected physician to the young community.

With all the new buildings going up, mostly frame, the danger of fire was apparent, and the citizens banded together to form a fire brigade. On May 17, 1869, fifty citizens founded the Pioneer Hook & Ladder Company. For several years it would only be a bucket brigade. With water to fight fire almost nonexistent, the little group of volunteers must have recognized their helplessness should a fire get out of control.

Water remained the number one problem. Water was still being hauled from the San Diego river. The artesian well near Spring Street (Broadway) furnished some water. In 1869 Horton sank an artesian well on Eighth between E and F and put up a windmill. Most houses had cisterns in which to catch rainfall, but this was more a hope than a reality, and was of use only during the rainy season. Soon other wells were dug and windmills sprang up here and there.

July 4, 1869, saw the first of many big celebrations in the new town. It was a good excuse to celebrate, not only the birth of their country, but the founding of their town, which they were now confident would become a great city. The celebration lasted for three days and nights. There were parades, fireworks and the usual speeches. The first day's festivities were held at the foot of Fifth Street at the steamship company's warehouse. The Declaration of Independence was read by Captain Matthew Sherman, and the oration of the day was delivered by William Cleveland, a prominent lawyer. A good time was had by all. On the second day, the celebration moved to Old Town where a horse race was the big event, and on the third day, all who could still be counted among the celebrants went to Monument City (Mexico-California border) to top off the occasion.

The only newspaper in the area had been the *San*

Fig. 22 Horton's first home, at
Tenth and G Streets

Diego Union. The first newspaper to be published in Horton's Addition was the *Weekly Bulletin*, which started publication on August 21, 1869. In 1873 it became a daily, and in 1881 after several mergers, became the *San Diego Sun*. In most instances its views and politics would be in opposition to those of the *Union*.

On September 18, 1869, General William S. Rosecrans paid another visit to San Diego. Arriving with a group of railroad officials, he was in town only one day and was royally entertained. While here he sold back to Horton the block that had been given to him a year before. The consideration was said to be $2000 in cash and two lots. Rosecrans was well satisfied with the deal, and after assuring residents that a railroad was a "certainty," he extended his best wishes and left on the steamer *Senator*. It would be interesting to know what he would have said, had he been told, while passing Point Loma, that some day a large part of the point would bear his name. General Rosecrans served in Congress as a representative from Northern California from 1885 to 1893. He died in 1898, the year Fort Rosecrans was established on Point Loma.

Horton, although married several times, had no children, but had an abundance of relatives and in-laws. He wrote enthusiastically to his family in Wisconsin, telling them about his new city, and urged them to come West and make their fortunes with him. Many of his relatives did just that. In the summer of 1869 his youngest sister, Lucy, arrived with her husband, W.W. Bowers. Bowers was later to become Collector of the Port, State Assemblyman, State Senator and Congressman. Soon after Bowers' arrival Horton announced plans for the Horton House, which was to be a lavish hostelry, "a palatial brick edifice," one of the finest in Southern California. His brother-in-law, W.W. Bowers, would be the architect and builder. The site of the Horton House was to be on D between Third and Fourth. This site received much criticism. In fact, an indignation meeting was called to protest the location (the first, but not the last, of many such indignation meetings to be held when location of public buildings was at issue.) The location was too far out and it was feared it would draw business away from lower Fifth and Sixth Streets, the "center" of town then being Fifth and H.

On September 30, 1869, Horton's parents, Erastus and Tryphena, arrived to make their home here. They had lived the past twenty years in Wisconsin. Now two of their six children, Alonzo

Fig. 23 The *Orizaba*

and Lucy, were living in San Diego. Horton had prepared a house for them at the corner of Tenth and H. Erastus Horton celebrated his eighty-second birthday on October 7. On the evening of the sixth a fine welcome was given them by the New San Diego Guard Band which marched to their home to serenade them, and wish the elder Horton a happy birthday. He was believed to be the oldest man in San Diego, which would indicate that California was still a young man's country.

In October Horton was chairman of a committee which met for the purpose of establishing a public cemetery in San Diego. It had become a matter of immediate and pressing necessity. At the meeting it was said that sanitary conditions would require that it be distant not more than four nor less than three miles from the shore of the bay. As a result, 200 acres were set aside for cemetery purposes. The name was selected by Mrs. Matthew Sherman. It would be known as Mount Hope Cemetery.

It was in November that Horton commenced the

building that would become known as Horton's Hall, located on the southwest corner of Sixth and F. It would cost $10,000, and was to be two-story, the lower floor to be used as a store and the upper as a meeting hall. Another two-story building he had under construction, on the northwest corner of Sixth and G, was to be used by him as an office, and by the Wells Fargo Express Company. This building became known as the Express Building. The upper floor, according to Horton, would be for a town library. However, it would be a few years before a library would materialize. San Diegans would have to argue about that for awhile. Probably the most significant event to occur during these first years, and one which would affect the entire development of the city, was the setting aside of 1400 acres as a public park.

Sometime in 1867 Horton asked the Board of Trustees, consisting of J.S. Mannasse, Thomas H. Bush and E.W. Morse, to set aside a large tract of land for park purposes while the land was cheap, selling for only a few cents an acre. His suggestion did not get far at first. However, Morse was interested, and he and Horton walked over land which might be available, and selected two 160 acre tracts they believed suitable. Then, they decided it should be larger, and selected a square tract, consisting of 1440 acres. On February 15, 1868, Morse presented to the Board of Trustees a resolution to set aside the tract "For the purpose of securing to the residents of the City of San Diego a suitable park." Before action could be taken, however, forty acres at the southwest corner had been sold for $175 to Isabella Carruthers. On May 26, after a new Board of Trustees had taken office, the ordinance was adopted. The new board was composed of Marcus Schiller, José Estudillo and Joshua Sloane. Their action was later ratified by a vote of the people.

The "square" park would have been bounded by Sixth, Twenty-Eighth, Ash and Upas. The Carruthers purchase removed the area bounded by Sixth, Eleventh, Ash and Date. Encroachments on the park land have been made by the San Diego High School and the Naval Hospital, but in the 1920s when it was suggested that San Diego State College should be given land in the park, the proposal was soundly defeated. Now any further attempt at encroachment, even the widening of a highway through the park, brings loud and vigorous protests.

In October 1869 the then trustees, James Mc-Coy, José Estudillo and Matthew Sherman, requested the state legislature to give consent to the dedication of the 1400 acres for a park. A strenuous attempt was made to reduce it by 480 acres on the east, but on February 4, 1870, the legislature passed an act approving the transfer of land as a public park. An attempt was made to repeal the act. Horton and others went to Sacramento and worked hard to preserve it, and the attempted repeal was defeated. However, no effort to improve the park was made for many years.

By 1869 it was apparent to even the die hards that South San Diego was going to supplant Old Town. Those who a year before were ready to make an affidavit that Horton was insane and should be committed to the state hospital at Stockton were beginning to wonder just who was crazy, Horton or they.

Many of the leading residents of Old Town had already moved to New Town, including E.W. Morse and Matthew Sherman. Even before Horton arrived, Sherman was grazing sheep on land he owned just east of Horton's Addition. In 1867 he built a home at Nineteenth and J. In 1869 he subdivided Sherman's Addition, which became known as East San Diego, and later as Golden Hill. Like Horton, he

donated land for a school, at Twenty-First and N, which became known as the East San Diego School. It opened in 1871 with fewer than twelve students. J.S. Mannasse had donated the lumber. Later, the Sherman School was built at Seventeenth and H, and then at Twenty-Second and Island. Sherman's interest in schools very likely stemmed from the fact that in 1867 he had married Augusta Barrett, the second school teacher to come to Old Town to teach at the old Mason Street School. E.W. Morse had married the first, Mary Chase Walker. Sherman later built his home at the corner of Twenty-Second and H. Part of that home still remains, incorporated in the building known as the Sherman Apartments at Twenty-Second and Market. E.W. Morse, who had become a close personal friend of Horton's, sold out his interests in Old Town in 1869 and moved to New San Diego to throw in his lot with Horton.

Much of Davis' Addition was now being incorporated into the new town, either through purchase from the owners, or at tax sales. By 1871, Davis owned only twenty-two lots, as against 150 in 1850.

The volume of business in San Diego in December, 1869, was reported to be $300,000, a sizable amount, and certainly not what would be expected from a "paper" town. Horton's gross receipts for the year 1869 were $85,000. He was on his way to becoming a millionaire. The *Union* reported in late 1869 "People are coming here by the hundreds, by steamer, by stage and by private conveyance... From a place of no importance, the home of the squirrel a few months back, we now have a city of 3000 inhabitants. Houses and buildings are going up in every direction... Every steamer from San Francisco averages 200 passengers for San Diego."

Some idea of the growth in Horton's assets is given from the property tax declarations he made in those first three years. As of July 8, 1867, he reported property valued at $235. On July 3, 1868, his assessed property valuation was $2,780, but in August of 1869 it had grown to $105,805. Included in the 1869 declaration of assets was a buggy valued at $100, and two gentle horses valued at $150.

The city Horton had dreamed of had come into being, and it had been built from scratch. This is not only a figure of speech, but was an uncomfortable reality. Local residents swore the first settler in these parts must have been the flea. San Diego was rapidly becoming known as the "Flea Capital of the West."

Chapter Six

New Town Becomes San Diego, 1870–71

The year 1870 started auspiciously with ground breaking ceremonies for the Horton House on January 1. Horton turned the first shovel of dirt. At his side was his faithful friend, E.W. Morse, and his brother-in-law, W.W. Bowers, who would be in charge of building. Many of those who witnessed the ground breaking swore they would never live to see the day when the hotel would be filled, or even completed, the plans were so grand for the little town. January also saw the formation of the Chamber of Commerce, but not until Horton and the *San Diego Union* had engaged in a battle of words, as well as action.

The *Union*, published weekly in Old Town, was beginning to feel some competition from the *Bulletin*, published in New Town. The *Union* declared the *Bulletin* was

"...the mouthpiece of six or eight leading citizens...From the date of its first appearance it has been the special organ of Mr. A.E. Horton and has been noteworthy only for the publication of some two columns per week of the most remarkably ungrammatical sentences under which types have ever writhed...Two weeks ago that paper contained a bombastic article suggesting the establishment of a Chamber of Commerce in San Diego. We believed this proposition to be ridiculous and calculated to make our community the laughing stock of the state...The remarks of the Union mortally offended the selfconceit of the half dozen persons referred to and one of them (Mr. Horton) set out poste haste for our office to discontinue his advertisement."

At the same time, Horton had asked for and paid up his bill. The *Union* continued

"We are obliged to Mr. Horton for the prompt payment of his little bill, as money is always acceptable in a newspaper office; yet we grieve to lose his valuable advertising patronage. We received the large sum of $40 per year for the insertion of his card and the withdrawal of that sum from our regular receipts at this time will seriously embarrass our business. But really we cannot believe the kind old gentleman is in earnest about this matter. He possibly was fretting over the location of the Court House."

Horton lost no time in rounding up support, not only for the opposition newspaper, but for a Chamber of Commerce. On January 20 eight persons had met at Sixth and F in the store of David Felsenheld to form a Chamber of Commerce. At the close of the meeting a resolution was passed that the *Bulletin* would be the "official organ" of that body. Aaron Pauley was elected president and Horton the treasurer. Among other matters discussed was the need for a competing steamship line, railroad promotion, and harbor improvements and fortification.

Fig. 24 Horton's Hall, Sixth and F Streets

After the Chamber of Commerce became an accomplished fact the *Union* hastened to assure its readers that it really never was opposed to a Chamber of Commerce, only that it believed it was too soon for one—there wasn't any business in San Diego. To which Horton and the founders of the Chamber of Commerce had a ready reply: That was the reason it was so badly needed!

At the same time, Horton was also having a running argument with the *Union* and with Old Towners as to the location of a courthouse. The "courthouse" then was located in rented rooms in the Whaley House in Old Town. As early as June 23, 1869, the *Union* had said

"This county is $90,000 in debt and there is not a decent public building in it. A Court House is a public necessity and must be put up at once. If the Board of Supervisors will not take hold and put it up then we shall call upon A.E. Horton to go at it and if ever Horton starts in, the house will go up without delay . . . In the meantime our friend Horton can sell a few corner lots and gather up his loose change so as to commence at once if the Supervisors fail to act wisely and well."

And in September, 1869, the Grand Jury said,

Fig. 25 Fifth and D, 1873, showing the Horton Bank Building under construction at Third and D

"Whoever heard of a county without a Court House or public building?"

By January, 1870, the need for a courthouse and jail, especially a jail, had become urgent. Horton first offered to the Board of Supervisors as a gift, Block 212 as a site for a courthouse. This is the block bounded by Third, Fourth, Cedar and Date. Old Towners immediately objected to a site in New Town, so far away. Even New Towners objected to this site, way up on a hill and completely inaccessible. It was always said Horton had great vision—just how true this is can be seen when some sixty years after the offer of this site city planners presented to San Diego the Cedar Street Mall Plan. The plans proposed that all city and county buildings would be grouped along Cedar Street from the park to the waterfront. Except for the City-County Administration Building on the waterfront, this plan was rejected by the voters in another dispute over location of public buildings.

In addition to a courthouse, schools and churches, Horton wanted a library for his town. He had this in

Fig. 26 Fifth Street, 1876, looking
south to Horton's Wharf

mind when he built the Wells Fargo Building, known as the Express Building, at Sixth and G. In 1869 he made a deal with Hubert Howe Bancroft, the historian and San Francisco book dealer, to trade him the block bounded by Third, Fourth, B and C in exchange for 600 books. Horton placed a valuation on these books of $2000 and intended them to be used as a nucleus for a city library.

On February 7, 1870, a group of citizens met at the First Baptist Church and formed the "Horton Library Association," with the expectation of the gift of books from Horton. Monthly dues were to be fifty cents. It was soon learned that it was all a misunderstanding. Horton did not intend to donate the books, he would sell them for $1000, one-half of what he valued them and payment could be made from the dues. As a result, a squabble developed, another meeting was called, and the name changed to "San Diego Library Association." Horton kept his books. For the time being the new library association, having no books, quietly went out of existence.

Also in February, and on Washington's Birthday, gold was discovered in Julian. Logically, the mine was named the Washington Mine. For awhile it looked as though another Gold Rush had started, with prospectors arriving on every boat and stage, stopping in San Diego only long enough to purchase picks and shovels and then head for the hills. There was even a threat that Julian, instead of San Diego, would become the county seat. However, within a few years the quantity and quality of gold ore fell off and the cost of mining became too great. The mines, one by one, were closed.

Horton's Hall, on the southwest corner of Sixth and F, was completed in May, 1870 and became much in demand for lectures, concerts and entertainments as it was the only theatre or public meeting hall. The theatre, seating 400 persons, was on the second floor and contained a stage sixteen by thirty-two feet. Downstairs was a roller skating rink. Later, the downstairs became a store building. Horton's Hall was also used as a church. At one time it was being used by both the Presbyterians and the Catholics, an expression of early ecumenicalism.

The opening of Horton's Hall on May 9, was a "Grand Concert and Dramatic Entertainment" for the benefit of the Pioneer Hook & Ladder Company. The concert was given by a local chorus which sang "with great enthusiasm," and the dramatic entertainment consisted of a two part drama depicting San Diego in 1870 and as it would be in 1880 "after the railroad from San Francisco had arrived." Admission was $1.00 for adults and fifty cents for children. Two hundred and fifty dollars was raised toward the purchase of a fire truck that would cost $800.00. Subscriptions were taken for the balance, Horton contributing $50.00. But it would be October before the truck was built. In the meantime, the bucket brigade carried on.

June 9, 1870, was another red letter day for New Town. On that date a group of prominent citizens got together to form a company for the transaction of a general banking business in New San Diego. These men were A.E. Horton, Bryant Howard, E.W. Morse, J. Nash, J.M. Pierce, M. Sherman, A.M. Hathaway, C. Dunham and W.H. Cleveland. It was to be known as the Bank of San Diego, with a capital of $100,000. A.E. Horton was elected president, James M. Pierce, vice president, and Bryant Howard, treasurer. Even the *Union* greeted this news enthusiastically, stating "This is another indication of the growth of our city. The bank will be a great convenience to our business community."

And a convenience it must have been, for up to that time there had been no bank in San Diego. This meant citizens were obliged to carry large amounts of money on their person, or keep it in safes, or hide it in their homes, at a risk of theft or hold-up. Coin, of gold and silver, was generally used—paper money being regarded with some suspicion. Money was often buried for safekeeping and it was not uncommon to see a bag of gold still bearing signs of dirt and dust from having been recently "dug up." In those days, it could be the literal truth when a person said "I'll have to dig up the money." The bank opened in one of Horton's buildings, on Sixth Street, between J and K.

Horton, the most affluent person in town, still kept his money in a bank in San Francisco, carrying it back and forth by ship in a satchel. His checks and drafts were passed from hand to hand and used as cash. Proud of his strength, Horton liked to tell of the time he returned from San Francisco with a satchel of gold, which appeared to be just an ordinary traveler's bag, and was approached at the steamer landing by a porter who offered to carry it for him. Horton asked if a two-bit tip would be enough. The man indicated that would be fine. He took the satchel from Horton and it dropped with a thud to the ground. The poor man could barely lift it! Horton thought this was very amusing.

Horton kept as much as $40,000 in gold coin in his safe at a time. He said there were times when "I took in so much money I didn't know what to do with it." Often coin and checks cluttered his desk because he did not have time to gather it up and put it away. Horton soon resigned as president of the bank. He said he was taking in more money in his real estate business than the bank was from all its depositors.

In spite of its differences with Horton, the *Union* finally had to admit that New Town was taking over and soon would become the county seat. So, on June 24, 1870, it moved to a new office at Fourth and D on the east side of the plaza. Still a weekly, its first issue in New Town was on June 30. It was now on the side of New Town, and of Horton, after having come to the conclusion that "If you can't beat 'em, join 'em." It possibly helped, too, when Horton promised to give it his advertising again if it would move to New Town. The *Union* must have prospered in its new location, because on March 20, 1871, it became a daily, boasting 400 subscribers.

By summer, 1870, the Horton House was well on its way to completion. It was described as "mammoth" and as "the largest building in Southern California." Horton had been paying his workmen partly in cash and partly in lots. Even so, and because of other building projects he had going on, he found himself running short of cash. The cost of the building was estimated to be $125,000. The furniture would require another $25,000, and this in cash, because San Francisco furniture dealers were not interested in taking San Diego lots in payment. Horton sent his brother-in-law, Bowers, to San Francisco to see what he could do about financing the furnishing of the hotel. Bowers visited banks and financiers with no luck. Finally, he found a furniture dealer who was far ahead of his time—he was willing to sell Horton furniture on time payments, something unheard of in those days. At about this time, as the Horton House was nearing completion, Western Union was seeking a subsidy in order to bring its line to San Diego. It wanted a guarantee of $8,000 worth of business within three years. Subscriptions were taken among the businessmen, and although twenty-three individuals and firms subscribed, it fell far short of the required amount. Finally Horton came to the rescue with a $5000 guarantee and in return was to receive one-half of the company's earnings for three years. In August the line was completed.

On August 20, at 10:45 a.m. the first wire was sent from San Diego to San Francisco.

San Diego sends greetings to San Francisco. Our telegraph is completed today, and we rejoice to be in direct contact with the rest of the world. Now give us the railroad and we will depend upon our natural resources and individual enterprise for the rest.
A.E. Horton.

The first message to be received was from Bowers telling of the furniture dealer who was willing to sell on time payments. Horton's reply came right back: "Take the furniture." Within a few weeks the first shipment of furniture arrived on the *Orizaba* with others to follow. The completion of the hotel was now assured. The day was saved and hope revived.

In August, just when he was busy with the hotel and Western Union and many other problems, Horton suffered an accident. He was driving on Seventh Street when his horse became frightened and ran away, tipping over the buggy and throwing Horton to the ground. He suffered a fractured right ankle. The *Union* reported "Dr. Huffman was sum-

Fig. 27 Western Union Telegraph, 1876, on the corner of Fifth and D Streets, decorated for the Fourth of July

Fig. 28 The Horton house was often
        called "palatial" and
        contained 100 rooms

Fig. 29 Charles S. Hamilton

moned to reduce the fracture and extract small fragments of bone. The operation was extremely painful but Mr. Horton refused the aid of chloroform or stimulants, bearing the pain without the slightest murmer. Mr. Horton's fine constitution and strictly abstemious habits are very much in his favor... We sincerely hope that San Diego will not long be deprived of the active labors of our most energetic and public spirited citizen." The injury did not slow him down for long and he was soon hobbling about. He had to be in fine fettle for the opening of the Horton House.

October 10, 1870, saw the hotel's gala opening. Residents agreed it was a veritable palace. Its 100 rooms were all furnished "in best style." Walnut Victorian, the grandest of the time, with marble top tables and washstands were in each room. All rooms were richly carpeted, lighted with gas, and supplied with fresh soft water. Half of them were warmed by steam heaters and "every one made wholesome and cheerful by the loveliest of sunshine some part of the day." Another unheard of luxury was that each room was connected with the office by a bell. The hotel also had "a magnificent view of harbor, ocean, islands, mountains, city and country." This view was especially compelling when seen from its observatory which held fifty people. The building was two and a half stories in height. On the first floor, near the dining room, were twenty rooms designated especially for invalids. The dining room was forty by sixty feet and "afforded a feast of beauty to the eye and more substantial and varied satisfaction to the 'inner man'." There were also a reading room, bar, billiard room, a ladies' parlor, and a sumptuous bridal suite, located at the extreme end of the second floor, facing west on Third Street.

Gas was piped into the hotel from a pneumatic gas works at the rear of the building. Water was supplied by a well fifty-five feet deep under the building. A tank held 7000 gallons and could supply 2000 gallons of water per hour, more than sufficient to supply the needs of the hotel. Water was piped into each room and miraculously furnished both hot and cold water! For the safety of the guests, 200 feet of hose were placed on each floor as protection against fire. They were assured the hotel was "fireproof."

The first manager of the Horton House was S.M. Churchill. The first clerk was a young man by the name of George W. Marston, age twenty, who arrived October 24 with his family from Ft. Atkinson, Wisconsin. Along with Marston was another contingent of Horton's family and friends from Wisconsin. Young George's father had known Horton in Wisconsin and had heard about this new town he had established in southern California. He and several other families came out together to see for themselves. If they liked what they saw, they would stay. Fortunately for San Diego, they did. The same day of his arrival, young George was employed as a clerk at the Horton House. He stayed on only long enough to get acquainted and then went to work for A. Pauly and Sons, the largest general merchandise store, and then later for Joseph Nash. He and his partner, Charles S. Hamilton, would then buy out Nash and start their own store. Marston later said that the first guests who arrived at the Horton House were a varied and interesting lot, Spanish, Mexican, soldiers, mining men, with the usual number of adventurers, "fast buck" operators and speculators sprinkled in. The latter of these individuals Horton tried to discourage from coming. When they did he made sure they did not stay long. He refused to sell land to them and when they discovered how tightly Horton held the reins of the little community, and that he was no "wheeler-dealer," they left for greener pastures.

In order to assure that his guests would always have a place to sit and enjoy the sun, Horton set apart the half block across from the hotel and designated it a plaza. He built a small fountain, placed benches around it and enclosed it with a hedge.

The opening of the Horton House served as a "shot in the arm" for the young city and gave great impetus to bringing new business and new residents to San Diego. Within ninety days after it opened, it was filled to capacity and by the end of the year Horton was again prosperous. The San Diego Union reported enthusiastically "Horton has met the great need of our young city. He did it by building and keeping a first class hotel; and I assert that the Horton House has done more for San Diego than all other improvements combined."

What was bringing people to San Diego? There were no factories, no farms, no timber, no water, no business, no jobs. The answer still was climate. The news had reached the North, South, Middle West and East, and even Europe, that here in Southern California could be found the best and most equable climate in the world, conducive to good health and longevity—worth more than gold or diamonds.

About this time, Horton acquired a badly needed secretary to help him in his office, to keep his records and accounts straight, as well as to gather up the money that was otherwise likely to lie around. He was Jesse Aland Shepherd, a native of England, who arrived in the United States at the age of fifteen and was apprenticed as a printer. In 1848 he went to Ft. Atkinson to work on *The Wisconsin Chief*. He married Fidelia Kinney, a first cousin of Horton's. His health had never been good, and when other Ft. Atkinson residents announced plans to go West, he and his wife decided to go along and try their fortune in cousin Alonzo's new town. Upon his arrival, in 1870, Horton employed Shepherd as a confidential assistant, at a salary of $100 a month, a post he held until his death in 1877. The name J.A. Shepherd, either as a notary or witness, appears frequently on deeds and documents during that period. He is not to be confused with the Jesse F. Shepard, spiritualist, musician and writer, who built Villa Montezuma and had San Diego agog in the late 1880s.

After the Horton House was completed and functioning, Horton took upon himself another project, that of securing some steamer competition. Ben Holladay, owner of the *Orizaba*, had a monopoly. He was charging $15 a ton for freight and $60 round trip for passengers. When approached by Horton to see if he would reduce these fares, he said, "Mr. Horton, I am running these steamers to make money and I am not going to put freight or passenger rates down." To which Horton replied "Then I shall have to do the best I can. I will put on an opposition line if I can find a steamer."

"Well, you do it if you can, and be damned!"

Holladay had not counted on the likes of Horton. Horton contacted George Wright, owner of the steamer *William Tabor*, which had just come around the Horn. He agreed to guarantee Wright one-half of the business that was going to Holladay, providing his freight rates would be $9 a ton and passenger fares $30 round trip. Wright wondered how Horton could be sure he could make good his promise. "I am employing in San Diego 100 men. I will tell them if they don't support the opposition line, their time is out and they can go wherever they can do better." Horton also assured Wright he would have no trouble convincing businessmen to use the new line because they were already unhappy with the old one. He was right, except for one firm, McDonald and Gale, partners in a general merchandise store, who failed to go along with the boycott of the old line. So, Horton told his workmen that if they traded there, their pay would be stopped. This, along with other residents who wanted to support the cause, was enough to make McDonald and Gale knuckle

under within two weeks. The *Tabor* had *all* the business, and the natural result of a lowering of fares and rates brought a huge increase in business.

Holladay was forced to go to Wright and ask how much he wanted to pull the *Tabor* off. Wright's price was $300,000, or $100,000 for one year's inactivity, but in any event he would have to first see Horton.

Fig. 30 Jesse Aland Shepherd who became Horton's secretary

"What, has Horton got anything to say about this?"

"Yes"

"The hell he has! Well, send for Horton!"

Horton went to San Francisco but refused to go to see Holladay. Holladay would have to come to see him at his hotel.

"Horton's pretty damned independent, isn't he?" Holladay went to see Horton.

Horton insisted that rates must remain the same, and on a guarantee they would not be raised. When Holladay saw Horton was not to be daunted, and would continue to hold out, he gave in and signed on Horton's terms. Wright was paid $100,000 and pulled the *Tabor* off the run.

The year 1870 was now coming to a close. It had been an eventful and prosperous one for the little community. The assessed valuation of real estate in the city was now $2,282,000 and of personal property $141,252. The national census of 1870 gave San Diego a population of 2301, although residents claimed 3000 was a more accurate figure. There were 915 occupied houses and sixty-nine business buildings. There was no question but that the town was growing into a city. Still there was no courthouse, and Old Town was the county seat, but not for much longer. The struggle for supremacy had been raging during the year, starting on July 9 when the Board of Supervisors ordered the removal of the county records from Old Town to New San Diego. They had not reckoned with the wrath of the Old Towners. A series of events began that sounds like a script written for the Keystone Kops. Judge Morrison, of the District Court, ruled that the clerk should make all writs issued from his court returnable in Old Town. Then, Judge Thomas H. Bush followed suit for his County Court, directing the sheriff to use force if necessary to prevent the removal of the records. A posse was called to aid the Sheriff. The next day the *Union* reported "The Crisis upon us: The secession of Old Town from San Diego...The cloud which has been hanging over so long has at length broken and this once happy land is now the scene of internecine strife. Old Town has seceded."

In September, Judge Bush removed the three supervisors and replaced them with three of his own choosing. It was asked, on what authority had he done this? In the meantime, Old Town had brought suit to restrain the transfer to New Town. On January 27, 1871, the Supreme Court of California ruled against Old Town concerning the removal, and held that Judge Bush had no authority to remove the Board of Supervisors. One of the

Fig. 31 On the evening of April 3, 1871 San Diego County records were removed from Old Town's Whaley House.

staunchest defenders of Old Town was the County Clerk and Recorder, George A. Pendleton. Pendleton died March 3, 1871, and the old, and legal, Board of Supervisors then appointed Chalmers Scott, a young attorney, to these offices and directed him to move the furniture and records to South San Diego. Pending a decision on the site for a new courthouse, the Board leased from Horton a part of the Express Building, Sixth and G, for one year at $95 per month. The lower floor became the courtroom, and two rooms upstairs were for the County Clerk. This building was then designated as the Courthouse of San Diego County. Horton still maintained his office in this building.

On the evening of April 3, Scott carted all the county records from the Whaley House into waiting express wagons, and the next morning was ready for business in New Town. This was not done surreptitiously as some writers have indicated. On March 29 Judge Morrison, having capitulated, had ordered all records moved to New or South San Diego, and the Board of Supervisors to provide necessary offices. Judge Bush did the same for his court. Thus, although the move may have been made at night to avoid interference from wrathful bystanders, it was not done illegally.

Daniel Cleveland later said Scott had moved the records "before the people at Old Town knew or

Fig. 32 San Diego merchant
Thomas Whaley and family

even suspected that such an attempt was being made. Great was their surprise and indignation the next morning when they learned of the great outrage that had been perpetrated upon them, but it was too late."

The *Union*, on April 4, reported "The new Court House building is being put in order with expedition. The County records were all brought over yesterday and are now safely housed." The *Bulletin* reported "A peaceful transition, agreeable to matured plans, the County Records and all the archives of San Diego County passed quietly and honorably from the oldest city in California to its young but lusty neighbor. It was inevitable." The most unhappy person no doubt was Thomas Whaley, who was left without a tenant, and was unable to collect the rent for the balance of his lease which ran until August 12.

On April 5 Judge Morrison officially opened court in New Town. Even Judge Bush must have been won over, for he soon built a fine home for himself at Sixth and A, later the site of the First Congregational Church, and his wife became a teacher at the B Street School. On April 14, 1871, the South San Diego Post Office officially became the San Diego Post Office. Now, Horton's town was no longer New Town, South San Diego, or New San Diego, it was San Diego!

Chapter Seven

The Scott Boom and Bust, 1871–73

After his block on Cedar Street had been rejected as a site for a courthouse, and when it was apparent that the county offices would be moved to New Town, Horton offered to sell Horton's Hall to the county for $10,000—his cost. It had been estimated that the cost of a new courthouse and jail, including land, would be about $47,000. This offer of Horton's seemed to many to be a good idea. The *Union* came out enthusiastically for this more economical plan, saying that Horton's Hall was ideal for the purpose. It was centrally located, fireproof, of excellent construction, and could be easily adapted for the need. A jail could be built separately for about $5000.

However, the Board of Supervisors turned down this suggestion. Then Horton offered a site, free to the county, at D (Broadway) and Front. He owned the east half of Block L, bounded by Front, Union, D and C. This was the boundary of Horton's Addition. The west half was in Middletown, and the owners were S.S. Culverwell, Jeff Gatewood, and others, who likewise agreed to donate it to the county. These gift deeds were accepted by the Board of Supervisors on April 15, 1871, exactly four years after Horton first stepped ashore at San Diego.

The deed to the Middletown half was without reservation. However, Horton's deed stipulated that the property could be used only for county purposes and that in default of such use the property would revert to and become the property of his heirs, just as if the deed had never been made. In 1938 when the county was considering several sites for a new courthouse, which might result in giving up this block to other uses, this stipulation was called to the attention of the Board of Supervisors. Suit was brought to Quiet Title, and as a result the county allegedly paid $25,000 to Horton's heirs for quit claim deeds.

William Jorres was selected as contractor to build the new courthouse. The contract called for $43,012, payable in gold coin. However, by the time the building was completed, the actual cost was closer to $55,000. Jorres was sent to San Francisco to sell bonds to raise the necessary money. Finally the cornerstone was laid August 12, 1871, with Horton again officiating with the shovel. One of the speakers, Dr. E.D. French, said he "hoped the ill feeling which had existed up to that time between Old and New San Diego might be buried in the stone."

Soon after construction started, the inevitable title litigation began, this time over title to the Middletown half. It was resolved satisfactorily, but in the meantime there was concern about the courthouse going up on land under a title cloud. It was then discovered that the building was five feet inside the dividing line, and entirely in Horton's Addition.

Horton, too, had been subjected to numerous lawsuits over his title to the whole of Horton's Addition. Most were by dissidents, jealous over the emergence of New Town. All were spurious and got nowhere. Nevertheless, because of the questioned title, there were many incidents of land jumping. Claimants would arrive and put up a fence, but just as soon as a fence went up, angry crowds would arrive and tear or burn it down. The last such law suit, brought in September, 1870, was entitled Charles H. DeWolf vs. A.E. Horton. When this suit was resolved in Horton's favor, it was accepted with no further question. Horton's title was undisputed after February 23, 1872, when the State Legislature passed an act whereby all prior conveyances of land by the municipal powers of San Diego were legalized, ratified and confirmed.

The courthouse was completed and opened June 4, 1872, with a grand celebration and dedication ball. The building was described as "The most substantial and elegant Court House in Southern

California." It was of brick and plaster, 60 feet wide, 100 feet long and 48 feet high. Present day economy minded citizens should take note, this little building housed not only the courtroom and jail, but also the offices of the Treasurer, County Clerk and Recorder, Board of Supervisors, Sheriff, District Attorney and Assessor! This building, with additions in 1888, 1911 and 1927, would stand, and be used as a courthouse, for nearly ninety years. During the last years of its life it was again involved in heated disputes as to whether a new courthouse should be built on the same site or in a different location. Proponents of the same site won out, but by that time another whole block would have to be acquired to furnish adequate space just for the courts, jail and related offices.

Early in 1871 Horton announced plans to build a new home for himself on the block bounded by Second, Third, A and B. His residence at Tenth and G also covered a whole block, on which he had planted trees, shrubs and flowers to make it a much admired garden spot. Water came from the well on Eighth Street. At first it was thought that the soil here was unfit for anything except grain. Horton believed otherwise and was confident that with water there was nothing that would not grow here. He set about to prove his point. He began on the block (Second, Third, A and B) that became known as Horton's Garden. He put in a well and windmill and built a fine glass hothouse. He then planted just about every kind of tree, shrub, flower and vegetable known—and they all thrived. By the end of the year 1871 there were growing ninety different kinds of trees and plants, including eucalyptus and pepper trees, banana and other rare plants. Although he built a barn and stable on that block, he never built a home there. Perhaps the garden had proved more of an asset. It remained a show spot for a number of years, and was much enjoyed by visitors to the Horton House. Many of the fine plants and trees were transplanted from time to time to other locations. When the courthouse was completed, the jailor, a Captain Gordon, landscaped the grounds with choice plants taken from Horton's Garden.

In August, 1871, two days before ground was broken for the courthouse, Horton was chosen as the Republican candidate for State Senator. The Democratic candidate was James McCoy of Old Town, who had been sheriff and auctioneer at the time of Horton's New Town purchase. McCoy had been one of the active opponents of moving the courthouse to New Town. The election was in September, leaving only a short time for electioneering, but even so those few weeks saw a strenuous and bitter campaign. Horton carried San Diego but lost in San Bernardino and McCoy was elected. The outcome turned largely on the wrath of C.P. Taggart, then a prominent Republican, who had good reason for not liking Horton.

In 1870, the Board of Trustees had conveyed to Taggart and V.E. Howard city tidelands in payment for legal services in establishing city boundaries in connection with land titles. This brought immediate opposition from those who were opposed to the sale of tidelands. Horton was one of these. The anti-tidelanders brought suit to test the validity of the grant to Taggart and Howard. The Supreme Court upheld them, finding that no law existed authorizing the sale of the shore of the ocean and that title remained in the state. Therefore, Taggart and Howard were left empty handed, and their hopes of making a fortune from the future sale of the tidelands were dashed. Subsequently they conveyed their interest back to the city of San Diego "for the benefit of the schools." Since their interest amounted to nothing, the schools got nothing, but it was a magnanimous gesture. This controversy was raging at the time of the election, and Taggart threw his support to McCoy and urged other Republicans, especially in San Bernardino, to vote for McCoy instead of Horton.

Horton now had succeeded in transferring the county seat to his town, had been successful in securing a reduction in steamer rates, and was still confident that it would not be long before San Diego would be the western terminus for a great railroad. San Diegans had for years been living on hope and great expectations that a railroad would come to San Diego, only to have those hopes dashed when promises went unfulfilled. San Diego was not alone in striving for a railroad. In 1868 Frank and Warren Kimball purchased Rancho de la Nación for $30,000 and laid out the town of National City, in the firm belief that it, not San Diego, would be the terminus of a railroad. The Kimballs and Horton became rivals, competing against one another for new residents and a railroad, whereas actually what would prosper one would help the other. The Kimballs also built a wharf, completed in August, 1871, hopefully to be used to bring in the coal that would be needed for the railroad. Competing with San Diego and National City was Los Angeles. Los Angeles had no harbor and so adopted San Pedro, and soon established a short line railroad from San Pedro to Los Angeles, expecting it to connect with the Southern Pacific—after having agreed to a large subsidy to Southern Pacific if it would extend

Fig. 33 San Diego Courthouse, built
in 1872

its line to there. Los Angeles was confident that it, and not San Diego, would get the railroad first. San Diego had been more fortunate with its natural harbor. New residents could come from San Francisco to San Diego by ship more easily than they could get to Los Angeles by way of San Pedro.

Most visitors and new settlers arrived in San Diego by ship from San Francisco. The Golden Gate was the doorway to California. Ships coming around the Horn or from Panama stopped first at San Francisco or Monterey for customs and im-migration clearance. Passengers then went south either by ship or stagecoach. The ship was more comfortable and safer, as the stagecoaches were still frequently held up by bandits or Indians. On May 10, 1869, when the Central Pacific met the Union Pacific at Promontory, Utah, there was for the first time direct rail transportation from East to West. The new arrivals in San Francisco frequently came on south to what they had heard was a land of milk and honey. Of those who arrived first in Los Angeles, many were discouraged from going any further. Los Angeles residents were diligent in their efforts to keep people from going farther south by telling all kinds of discouraging tales of what they would find in San Diego. After all the discomforts of getting that far, many were content to settle down and go no farther.

46

Between San Diego and Los Angeles there was a stagecoach line run by Seeley and Wright. Stagecoaches left the Horton House daily, except Sunday, at 5:00 a.m., from Old Town at 6:00 a.m., arriving at San Juan Capistrano at 7:00 p.m. Passengers stayed there overnight, starting again at 4:00 a.m. and reached Los Angeles at 1:00 p.m. The fare was $10, one way.

John G. Capron, proprietor of a U.S. mail line, gave a tri-weekly service with four-horse coaches between San Diego and Tucson, a journey which took as long as five days and cost $90. These coaches were frequently accosted by Apache Indians. Other travelers from the East or South arrived by this stagecoach from Yuma. William Tweed ran a passenger and mail line to Julian three times a week. The fare was $7.00 up, and $6.00 down.

The *Orizaba* was the steamer that brought most new residents to San Diego in the early years. To say "My folks came down on the *Orizaba*" was about the same as saying "My ancestors came over on the *Mayflower*," except that the *Orizaba* made many more trips bringing in new residents. The *Orizaba's* first run from San Francisco was on January 10, 1865, and it continued to carry passengers and freight to San Diego until 1887. It was a sidewheeler and a coal burner, but carried sails, and was 246 feet long. Later a companion ship, the *Santa Rosa*, which was a bit larger, was put on the run. The *California* and the *Senator* were other ships making frequent runs between San Francisco and San Diego, a trip taking three days. At first a ship arrived every twelve days, later every six days. The cannon at the barracks would be fired to announce the arrival of a steamer, and then the whole town turned out to greet the newcomers. Horton was always the first aboard to extend a welcome. In the next day or two he would do a "land office" business. The skipper of the *Orizaba* was Captain Henry James Johnston. On one of his stops in San Diego he purchased sixty-five acres for $16.25, in what became Mission Hills. He did nothing with the land and it passed to his heirs. When it was subdivided it became known as Johnston Heights, located east of Witherby and south of Sunset Boulevard. In 1887 his daughter, Sarah Johnston Miller, built the Villa Orizaba on what became Orizaba Street. It had a commanding

view of the bay and was built partially from salvage wood and fixtures taken from the *Orizaba* when it was decommissioned. The house still stands, although modernized and altered in appearance.

As far back as 1854 San Diegans had begun talking about a railroad. In that year the San Diego and Gila Railroad was incorporated. Plans were for a railroad from San Diego to Yuma to join there with a line from the East. The Civil War came along, however, and that ended all prospects of a railroad for the time being.

In 1867 when General Rosecrans spoke enthusiastically to Horton about the prospects of a road to the East from San Diego, it gave encouragement to further hopes and rumors that the Southern Pacific was interested. In 1869, Frank Kimball of National City was in negotiation with the Memphis & El Paso (the Fremont line) raising hopes again that San Diego, or National City, would become the terminus for a line from Memphis. However, in 1870 Fremont, although receiving offers of European financing, was unable to get a grant of land from Congress and his plan failed. San Diego's hopes were again dashed, causing a minor depression, and Horton was obliged to keep more men busy to boost the economy along. During these early years, Horton built no less than fifty houses, in addition to his hotel, hall and office buildings. It was Horton who paid most of the expenses for city government from his own pocket. And it is estimated he gave away at least twenty-two blocks to city, county and churches.

Early in 1871 the Texas & Pacific Railroad had a request for a charter before Congress and San Diegans became excited, believing this might be the answer to their prayers. Horton hastened to Washington, D.C. and contacted Col. Thomas A. Scott, one of the organizers. (It may have already been noted that many of the organizers of railroads after the Civil War were high ranking retired army officers). Through Horton's friends and influence in Washington he was able to have incorporated in the bill a provision that work should commence simultaneously from Marshall, Texas, westward, and from San Diego, eastward.

On March 3, 1871, the bill passed both houses of Congress. The Texas & Pacific had received its Charter! San Diegans were jubilant! The *San Diego Union* reported that on the evening of March 3rd, "The City was ablaze with bonfires; houses were illuminated, fireworks set the sky aglow and the booming of 20 anvils in different parts of the city, the heavy roar of the cannon at Old Town, an inces-

Opposite:
Fig. 34 Frank Kimball

sant fusillade of crackers and Chinese bombs and the unearthly screech of half a dozen whistles, created such a din as San Diego never heard before."

This started another influx of boomers and speculators. On June 20, 1871, a large party of excursionists arrived from Chicago to investigate real estate investment possibilities. Soon all hotel rooms were overflowing. Lots which had been selling for $350, within a few days or weeks, were being sold for $1000. In the two months after passage of the railroad act Horton sold $83,000 worth of lots and in 1872 he sold $56,000 worth in ten weeks.

Horton lengthened his wharf to allow deep draft vessels to come in, and in 1872 sold it to the Pacific Mail Steamship Company. The company's first ship, the *Costa Rica*, arrived September 21, 1872.

After passage of the railroad bill an attempt was made to delay the start at the western end. A citizens' committee was quickly organized headed by Thomas L. Nesmith, and Horton was again sent to Washington. In March, 1872, while Horton was in Washington, his assistant, J.A. Shepherd, commented in his diary:

March 6: The news from Washington says no harm is meant to San Diego in Congress on the railroad "extension". All's well if it ends—in San Diego.
March 20: Blue is the color of public sentiment hereabouts...Railroad expectations seem vanishing in the distance like a dream when morning wakes us to realities.

On April 20, 1872 a fire devastated much of Old Town, which finally eliminated it as any competition, although by then most of its prominent residents had moved to New Town. Of this event, however, Shepherd's diary makes this laconic comment:

April 20: Nothing of unusual interest today, but not so at Old Town. The stillness has been broken there by a fire consuming three or four buildings.

The first stake in the survey for the Texas & Pacific was laid at National City on June 22, 1872. J.A. Shepherd rode out to represent Horton. The Kimballs were still certain the terminus would be at National City. San Diegans were equally certain it would be in their town. The tug of war went on.

In July Horton returned with a hopeful report. Nevertheless, delays and disputes over engineer-

Fig. 35 Captain Henry James Johnston

Fig. 36 Horton's second home
(right), Sixth and A Streets,
and "Little Pink School-
house" (left), Sixth and B
Streets

ing reports continued. Scott demanded that he should first receive all lands held by the old San Diego & Gila Railroad, as well as rights of way through the city and county, and waterfront rights of way. Finally Scott himself decided to come to San Diego. He and his party came by Union Pacific to San Francisco, then by the steamer *California* to San Diego. They landed at Horton's Wharf on August 26, 1872, and were greeted by a huge and delirious crowd, then driven in royal style to the Horton House where another large crowd had gathered in the plaza. Scott spoke to the crowd from a balcony of the Horton House. He assured them of a railroad "within five years." Other speakers told the audience what this would mean to San Diego. After an elaborate banquet at the Horton House, Scott was assured by the leading citizens that he could have all that he demanded. Scott's party sailed at midnight. They were in town less than twenty-four hours, but did not need longer to get all they asked for. San Diego agreed

to turn over 9000 acres, plus waterfront rights of way. Kimball offered as a subsidy half of National City, plus 11,000 acres. San Diegans went to bed confident that their city would be the southern terminus of a cross-country railroad.

Prosperity in San Diego swung like a pendulum depending on railroad news. By September Shepherd's diary showed that the pendulum now was on the prosperous side.

September 2: Real estate is in demand. Even the unbelievers are becoming converted to the possible success of our place.

By fall (1872) the railroad plans seemed to be going along well, with reports of activity at Marshall, Texas. In the meantime, Horton was busy with other activities. In November the *Union* reported: "Mr. A.E. Horton is indefatigable in his exertions to improve and build up this city. He scarcely finishes one enterprise before he starts another. He is now contemplating the erection of a brick block on D Street in the vicinity of the Court House. From present indication D Street will be one of the finest in the city." The building referred to was one to be at the southwest corner of Third and D known as the Horton Bank Block, which Horton said would cost $45,000 and would be used as offices for the Texas & Pacific. The next day, the

Union reported "Mr. Horton will commence the erection of a fine building at the corner of 6th and A which he probably will occupy when completed."

Horton had hit a financial peak at this time, and was confident that the future would be even better. He was by far the number one property owner in the county, as shown by the 1872 assessment rolls which listed the valuations of the top property owners as:

A.E. Horton	$124,971
John Forster	87,681
Louis Rose	36,330
Cave J. Couts	26,122
Bank of San Diego	20,000
Joseph Nash	15,720

Shepherd wrote in his diary at the time, "Wealth makes work as much as poverty. A rich man has no time to be idle. I don't speak from experience—only from association. Looking after Horton's Addition is no small task, especially when taxes are delinquent."

1872 was a presidential election year. Horton had been a "Black" Republican. Now he became a "Liberal" Republican. It was in that year the Democrats and the Liberal Republicans did an unprecedented thing, they joined together to back Horace Greeley against U.S. Grant who was seeking a second term. The "Straight" Democrats nominated a third candidate. In San Diego an association was formed known as "Friends of Greeley-Brown." In July, they held a great rally in front of the Express Building. The *Union's* reporter was on hand. "We have no hesitation in saying that the gathering was the most extraordinary one that has ever been witnessed in San Diego County. Here we saw in fraternal intercourse Democrats of the most intense prejudices and Republicans whose faith has been akin to bigotry—surely a more remarkable mixture than that of oil and water." Horton was elected president of the association and received cheers as he stepped on the platform. He returned thanks in a brief speech announcing his determination to support Horace Greeley as the man whose election would "restore peace, prosperity and fraternal feeling throughout the country." The vice president of the association was Col. Jeff Gatewood, first editor of the *Union*, who "always speaks eloquently" and who had been a lifelong Democrat. It was never truer than on this occasion that "politics makes strange bedfellows."

Grant was re-elected and by the time another election rolled around, Horton was back in the fold claiming he had never really left the Republican Party. If Horton could not get elected to public office, his brother-in-law, W.W. Bowers, was to be more successful. Bowers was elected to the State Assembly, serving in 1873-74, thus beginning a long and distinguished career in public office.

In March, 1873, the Hortons moved into their new home on the northeast corner of Sixth and A. It was a two story frame building, with a view of Coronado Islands, Point Loma, the bay, and even a glimpse of False Bay. It was "elegantly" furnished, contained both a parlor and a library, was lighted with gas, and water for its use was supplied by the well at the Horton House. Their home at Tenth and G, and that entire block, was sold to Thomas L. Nesmith who had arrived in San Diego in 1870 and succeeded Horton as president of the Bank of San Diego.

A reporter from the *Union* was given a tour of the Hortons' new home and described it thus:

"The Parlor is furnished with the new fashioned style of furniture known as the tan color, having black walnut frames and medallion figured silk tops. The curtains are a rich and heavy lace. The floor is covered with a fine medallion figured Brussels. A fine piano ornaments this room. The dining room is furnished with a beautiful walnut sideboard, an extensive table and other articles. Fruit pictures hang from the walls and a magnificent Brussels covers the floor. On the south side of the house is the library which contains a full set of books, one of the largest in the city."

Also on the ground floor were a kitchen, two pantries, closets, bathroom, wash room and kitchen range "all fitted up after the most approved style." There were three bedrooms with "fine closets" upstairs. The Hortons now had living with them one of Mrs. Horton's nieces, Amy Brown. On June 4, 1873, an advertisement appeared in the *Union* "Wanted—a woman to do the work for a family of 3 persons. Inquire of Mrs. Horton, cor. 6th & A Sts."

On April 21, 1873, the great day arrived for San Diego. It was ground breaking day for the railroad! Again, it was Horton who turned the first sod. "Ladies and Gentlemen: I regard this as the greatest honor the Pacific Coast could possibly confer on me." This little speech was greeted with cheers. Even Mr. Taggart was generous in his remarks: "Mr. Horton had commenced the City of San Diego and from that day to this it has gone ahead more rapidly than any other city of the Pacific Coast, and he has done more for it than any other man in it." Quite a speech for one who had been a bitter antagonist. Taggart let it be known, however, that he still didn't like Horton. The feeling was mutual. But Taggart felt Horton deserved

Fig. 37 Horton's Garden, looking
north, block bounded by
Second, Third, A and B
Streets

the credit for what was happening. The *Union*, too, praised Horton, "The one man on the Pacific Slope rightfully entitled to the honor of turning the first sod on the Texas and Pacific Railway is A.E. Horton, a man who believed in San Diego while it was yet unbuilt and who had proved his faith by his work."

Strangely enough, only a small crowd attended the ground breaking ceremony, which occurred without much advance notice. The *Union* reported "Yesterday, without noise, without ostentation, the work of construction of the California terminus of the Texas & Pacific Railway was commenced in this city. Thus, in a plain businesslike way the company has proceeded, step by step, until—almost before our people are prepared to realize the fact—the building of the railroad is actually going forward" In May, as a result of the influx of visitors and new residents, Horton proposed building a sixty room addition to the Horton House, at a cost of $10,000, to help meet the shortage of rooms in the city.

In July of 1873 Horton purchased for $10,000 the building at the northwest corner of Third and D known as the Veazie Building. It was occupied by the Commercial Bank of San Diego and the San Diego Water Company. The Commercial Bank was the second bank to open in San Diego. It was organized in 1872, but did not begin business until March of 1873. Horton was hopeful that this bank would occupy his new building across the street, then under construction on the southwest corner of Third and D. But, the directors of the new bank decided not to lease Horton's building. Instead they would erect their own bank building at Fifth and G, and in October began construction of that building. Horton, being rebuffed by the Commercial Bank, said he would open his own bank in his new building, in which he built what was claimed to be the strongest vault in California.

In September, Col. Scott went to Paris to sell his bonds in order to raise the necessary funds to complete the railroad. French bankers agreed to take the bonds. Since it would take a few days to iron out details before making delivery of the bonds, Scott and his party decided to go to London. While there, on September 18, 1873, "Black Friday" occurred, when the stock market crashed and the banking house of Jay Cooke & Co. failed. This caused the French bankers to have a change of heart, and when Scott returned on Monday, the deal was off. Scott returned to the United States a broken man, financially and in spirit. He telegraphed Horton: "I have lost the sale of my bonds and am a ruined man. I don't know whether I shall ever be able to get my head above water again. Do the best you can. I shall not be able to fulfill the contracts I have with you."

Only ten miles of road had been graded. Work stopped immediately. The real estate boom collapsed, the number of jobless grew, people left like rats off a drowning ship. The population in 1870 had been 2301. By 1873 it had grown to 5000. In a matter of a few months it had dropped to 1500. There was little business. Many buildings stood vacant and the atmosphere was one of gloom and doom. One wit said that after the boomlet burst he could have fired a cannon in the middle of the day right down D from Fifth and it would have disturbed only the serenity of the occasion. Horton was badly hurt financially. Many newcomers had purchased property with only a down payment and then were forced to leave town. Horton never turned down a plea for help. He returned their money and took back the property.

Of those who remained, there were those who were pleased with the turn of events. In later years they would be called "The Geranium Growers." They had come here for their health and to retire. They wanted peace and quiet, and with the failure of the railroad they could be assured of both.

Fig. 38 Horton Bank Block, Third and D, built 1873

Opposite:
Fig. 39 Horton Bank Block, renamed Union Building, 1900

Chapter Eight

Living on Climate and Great Expectations, 1874–79

The next decade in San Diego was a period of marking time. Those who were retired or who had come for their health were content to live on climate and savings they had brought with them. The boomers and speculators left. Others who remained stayed because they liked it here and, like Horton, were confident that because of its climate and bay San Diego would one day be a great city. They were willing to wait, time and again being buoyed up by promises of great things to come, meaning—a railroad. In the meantime it was an enjoyable little town, without a political boss, comparatively little wrangling, and with no class consciousness. There were no society "greats." Each individual was accepted for himself, without regard to his background or financial condition. It was a melting pot in which everyone had an equal chance to prosper or to fail.

What was San Diego like in the 1870s as a place to live, work and have fun? Waldo Chase has said in his *Memoirs* that one need only go to the well-known amusement center of Knott's Berry Farm to get some idea what San Diego looked like in the seventies. Without the discomfort of the dust and flies and fleas, one can wander down the recreated "Main Street" in Knott's Berry Farm and visualize somewhat how it must have been to live in San Diego in those early days. Fifth Street was "Main Street." The center of town was at Fifth and H (Market), and D (Broadway) was still "way out."

The fleas and the flies were ever present, a plague to be endured, and so was the dust which was even worse than the "smog" that worries us today. Shepherd's diary of September, 1872, gives some idea of his frustration:

"I wish the wind would postpone the sweeping of D Street until it rains, for sandpaper is hard writing material...Dust and flies! San Diego is flying in all directions. Tries one's patience and piety to write on sandpaper and whip flies off the end of your nose at the same time."

The hedge around the plaza was often so covered with dust that no green could be seen.

It was the custom to keep a feather duster by the door so one entering could dust his clothes and shoes. Even the churches kept a big feather duster handy. Housewives were never caught up with their dusting. When water became more plentiful, a horse-drawn cart, with a water barrel which emitted a spray of water, was used to sprinkle the streets, much to the delight of children who liked to be sprinkled too. This was but a temporary help and created mud which was equally as bad.

When heat and dust were not a problem, keeping warm was. Some of the more "elegant" homes were fortunate in having fireplaces, but most depended solely on the kitchen stove for heat. The only sidewalks were wooden planks laid on Fifth Street from the waterfront to C. They were twelve feet wide and raised out of the dust and mud. Overhangs on the buildings provided for shade and some protection from wind and rain. There was a complete absence of trees for shade. Only a few buildings were of brick, most of wood and of poor construction and hardly more than shacks. None were over two stories in height. Most of the buildings were concentrated along Fifth and Sixth Streets from the waterfront. A few houses extended up to Russ Hill where San Diego High School is today. Other buildings and homes dotted the landscape south and west of the courthouse in Davis' New Town and the Middletown additions.

Indians were still much in evidence around the city during the seventies, although "peaceful." There were a half dozen or so Indian camps or rancherias on the brush covered mesa north of B and east of Sixteenth. There was a large rancheria near Eighth and Date. At night, their chanting could be heard for miles, especially if there had been a death amongst them.

"El Capitan" claimed to be Chief of the

Fig. 40 Looking up San Diego's
Fifth Street in the 1879s

Diegueño Indians. He lived with his wife and several children near the army barracks in an old tent given him by the soldiers. He was frequently seen wearing a plug hat and a bright red shirt. He stated he was the owner of the entire "pueblo" and went about asking for handouts of twenty-five and fifty cents and did quite well, but not in his opinion well enough. He demanded that a judge sign an order requiring citizens to pay him "two bits" on demand. Finally, Judge Bush went along as a joke and fixed up an impressive document with seal and red tape which purported to authorize him to ask any and all merchants and businessmen for twenty-five cents a week. Many did pay to keep him happy, and perhaps hoping also to keep his people happy—and out of town. He continued to collect his "tax" until his death in 1875.

While Col. Jeff Gatewood was editor of the *Union*, he called the Indians "an excrescence upon the mesa and upon the government lands near the barracks, and they are no earthly use to themselves or to others." The local Indians were known as "Lo" and were not infrequently mentioned in the local press. One news account told of some

Indians who had lost their garments in a gambling bout, and "Lo stalked about in the altogether." This was too much for the decent, law abiding citizens, who demanded that "something" be done. Another report, "Four young squaws, the oldest not more than 15, got drunk yesterday and had a wrestling match on 5th Street."

Father Ubach, the beloved priest from Old Town, went about lovingly attending the Indians, helping to see that they had food and the bare essentials of life, and medical care if they would accept it. Ubach, who had come to Old Town in 1866, only a year before Horton arrived, became a great friend of Horton's and finally moved to New Town when St. Joseph's Catholic Church was established in 1875. A little frame church was built at Third and Beech on lots given by Horton. Before that, Father Ubach held Catholic services at Rosario Hall, on Arctic (Kettner) at F. He was loved not only by his own parishioners, but by all residents of Old and New Town, regardless of their religion.

Whereas Spanish had been the accepted tongue in Old Town, and the Americans who settled there were obliged to learn the language, now English was the common language. Mexicans had to learn English if they expected to work for or do business with the newcomers. Although New Town was at first bilingual, with the early residents learning some Spanish, by the seventies San Diego like all of California had become Americanized. The language and way of life of the Mexican population had been supplanted by American competitive enterprise.

What were San Diegans eating in the seventies? Food was not easy to come by in the town. Those who could sink a well or put up a windmill on their property were able to grow some vegetables and fruit, grapes and figs being the most common. Bananas were available when a ship arrived from Panama. There was not much beef because cattle were raised primarily for their hides. There was, however, plenty of mutton, as well as fish. In fact, it was said San Diegans lived on fish and climate. Most of the fishing was done by Chinese who sold it door to door, carried in baskets hung over their shoulders. The Chinese came to San Diego in the late sixties and early seventies after having completed work on the railroad in the north. In May, 1870, the Presbyterian Church started a Sunday School for the instruction of Chinese in the English language and religion. It met every Sunday at 2:00 p.m. There were seven pupils at the first meeting and it was said to be the pioneer Chinese school in Southern California.

In November 1872 Horton sold a lot on Third Street to Wo Sung & Co., a large importing house of San Francisco, which proposed to build a two story brick building and establish a branch in San Diego. These earlier Chinese were the nucleus of a larger contingent who would occupy a section in the eighties and nineties known as "Chinatown."

San Diego also had its own flour mill. It was by the whistle from the mill that residents set their clocks, just as they did later by the gas company's whistle.

By the mid seventies the San Diego Water Company, organized in 1872, was providing some water through pipes from its wells and reservoirs in Pound Canyon (Cabrillo Freeway). They set about drilling artesian wells and building reservoirs. The first water piped to the city was from a well at Eleventh and B. But most San Diegans still depended on Joe Tasker and Jake Hoke, who delivered water from their well at the southeast corner of First and B, at five cents a bucket or twenty-five cents a barrel. An advertisement for their product, in the Union of August 2, 1873, read: "If people will drink water, when it is recorded that the world was once drowned out by that element, let them get a good pure quality of it from Messrs. Tasker & Hoke who are filling orders promptly and at very reasonable rates." In spite of the guarantee of the "good pure quality" of the drinking water, one who remembered those early days said "First we boiled the water, then we strained it, then we boiled it again, then we drank something else."

In 1875 the water company went to the San Diego river for water and drilled a well at the foot of Sandrock grade, then pumped water up hill to a reservoir at the southwest corner of Fifth and Hawthorne. San Diegans were now assured of a "seemingly inexhaustible supply" of water. But before long another pumping station would have to be built in University Heights and one at Old Town.

There were times when San Diego had too much water. On January 18, 1874, a flood hit Old Town. Two ferries had to be put into operation to cross the river at Old Town. The only communication between San Diego and the outside world was by steamer and telegraph. The next year Congress appropriated $80,000 to channel the river into False Bay (Mission Bay), which had been attempted in the 1850's. Since then, silt and sand had washed down making the Derby Dyke inadequate so that the river was flowing back into San Diego Bay and destroying the harbor. Work on the new channel was completed in 1877.

San Diego now had a fire engine. In 1872 San Diego Fire Engine No. 1 became the successor to the Pioneer Hook & Ladder Company and in April, 1874, the first fire plug was installed at Fifth and D. The "fire department" still consisted of local residents, including many of its leading citizens, who volunteered their services and scrambled to duty whenever the alarm was sounded.

On August 3, 1874, at a meeting of the City Board of Trustees, the Treasurer's Report showed a balance on hand as of August 1 in the City Treasury of $6,491.96. It was reported that Horton offered to lease a room in Horton's Hall to the city for two years, at twenty-five dollars a month, as a City Hall, which was accepted. Prior to that, the Board of Supervisors had been allowing the Board of Trustees to meet in the Jury Room in the Courthouse. It was also reported at this meeting that the Fire Department wanted authority to purchase a hose and cart, and that a very fine hose could be obtained for $269. Authorization was given to spend $500 for the hose and cart.

How were these transplanted Americans, having come from more populous areas of the country, making a living in this far away corner of the United States where there was no industry, no business and not even many people? The chief "industries" in the mid seventies were wheat, wool, honey, whale oil, dried fish, hides and salt. The cattle ranches were still raising cattle for their hides, to be shipped to the East. The great salt beds in the south bay were the source for the salt used in preparing the hides and drying fish. La Punta Salt Works, established in 1871, covered sixty acres along the south bay, and by the eighties was supplying all the salt used in Southern California. Wheat was plentiful, most of it being shipped to the North and East. The many sheep grazing on the mesas were a source of wool and mutton. Honey became a major industry. Beekeeping was introduced in San Diego County by J.S. Harbison in 1869 on his homestead in Harbison Canyon near Alpine. By 1874 San Diego County was first in the state in quantity produced. In 1875 Harbison shipped thirty-three carloads of honey to the East. The sagebrush which was everywhere and considered a nuisance and of no value to the early settlers, proved to produce the finest "wild" honey. The olive industry was one of the oldest. Cuttings were brought by the Franciscan Fathers and thrived as they did not need much water. The olives were used mainly for oil. The site of one of the first olive groves later became a large orchard and canning plant. Now the California Department of Transportation occupies the location in Old Town.

At first, in the city, there were only the service trades: hotels, rooming houses, grocery stores, lumber yards, building supplies, general merchandise stores, harness and blacksmith shops, Chinese laundries and the ubiquitous saloon. All the lumber, goods and merchandise for the shops, had to be brought in by ship. W.W. Stewart built a warehouse at the foot of Fifth, near the wharf, where grain, hides and other products were stored for shipment from San Diego. The census of 1871 listed eighty-five different occupations including farmers, miners, 22 physicians, 20 saloon keepers, 33 lawyers, 1 gentleman, 1 capitalist, and 1 windmill builder. It is interesting to note that at this time San Diego had more lawyers than saloon keepers. Lawyers and "judges" were prolific in the early days, seeming to literally come out of the woodwork. They did come from far and near, many for their "health" after deciding San Diego would be about as far away as they could get from their former haunts. Some were fine lawyers and added much to the community. Others, it is just as well to forget when the history of the Bench and Bar is written.

At the time of the Scott Boom, dealing in real estate seemed to be the leading occupation. Horton was no longer the only one in that business. Almost everyone who was not in a trade went into real estate. As a matter of fact, it seemed to many in the early seventies that "everybody here was in the real estate business."

Business advertisements in the seventies give a good indication of some of the firms that were successful enough to afford newspaper advertising. The Big Shoe Blacksmith & Wagon Shop was located at the corner of Eighth and J. The United States Restaurant was near the Pacific Mail Steamship Company's Wharf (formerly Horton's) at the foot of Fifth. Meals were twenty-five cents and "can be obtained at all hours. Sleeping rooms also available." Schneider & Abegg, Booksellers & Stationers, were in a new brick building on Fifth, near F. John G. Capron's Stages (U.S. Mail Line) "leave for Yuma Sunday, Tuesday and Thursday, 10 a.m." Dr. Fred Ephrat, Deutscher Arzt (German doctor) Physician, Surgeon and Accoucheur, on Fifth at corner of H (Market). One of the larger advertisers was Felsenheld's Brick Store, Sixth & F, which emphasized women's clothing. By far the most "ads" were by those in General Merchandise. Besides Felsenheld's, some of these included Steiner & Klauber Co., Seventh & I; A. Pauly & Son, Horton

Fig. 41 Commercial Bank Building,
Fifth and G Streets in 1870s

House Plaza, "Goods Cheap;" Loewenstein & Company, Commercial Bank Building, "Dry Goods, Clothing, Fancy Goods, etc;" Gordon & Hazzard, Sixth & H and Hamilton & Marston's, Fifth & J. J.S. Mannasse & Company, dealt not only in general merchandise, but also in "real estate, horses, cattle and mules."

In 1873 George W. Marston and Charles Hamilton, who had been clerking for Joseph Nash, bought Nash's mercantile business for $10,000. They remained partners for the next five years. In 1878 Marston opened his first store at the northwest corner of Fifth and D. The grand opening was on August 8, 1878. The first day's sales amounted to only $10.50. Soon Marston realized he was too far up town, and so moved his business to a location on Fifth between G and H, later to the corner of Fifth and F. The hours at Marston's store were 8:00 a.m. to 9:00 p.m. Hamilton's first grocery store was at Fifth and G.

There were two banks, The Bank of San Diego, on Sixth between G and H, and the Commercial Bank, corner of Fifth and G. In 1879 these two banks merged to become the Consolidated Bank of San Diego, located in the old Commercial Bank Building.

The Pioneer Drug Store, operated by Legare Allen, was located at Fifth and F. "The Fashion" on Fifth Street claimed "This popular and elegant Saloon is the best in the city." "The Gem" at Seventh and K advertised "Wines, liquors & cigars. Also ice constantly on hand."

There were several private schools. In the early

seventies the three Gunn sisters, Sarah, Lucy and Anna, conducted a small private school at Ninth and G for some of the small fry whose parents could afford this luxury for their children. This school soon went out of existence when two of the sisters married George W. Marston and Charles S. Hamilton, and the other married Major Lee Utt. In 1873 the San Diego Seminary, a boarding and day school for boys and girls, was opened on Second, between D and E, by the Rev. D.F. McFarland, who had been head of a seminary in Santa Fe, New Mexico. In the late seventies two sisters arrived from Boston to start a "Kindergarten," a new method of teaching which had originated in Germany and was only recently introduced in the United States. Sarah Henrietta Curtis and Delia Augusta Curtis had taught in the East and in northern California, and now hoped to introduce their system in San Diego. They established a Kindergarten on Sixth Street, just north of the B Street School.

Fig. 42 City Hall, early 1900s
(Commercial Bank Building
with two stories added)

Fig. 43 San Diego baseball team members pose for a group photograph

Fig. 44 The old Point Loma Lighthouse was a frequently visited place during Sunday outings

And what were early residents doing for entertainment? San Diegans have always been fortunate in having opportunities for recreation and entertainment, many at no cost. Fishing and hunting were fine at False Bay (Mission Bay), which was also a paradise for duck hunters. Rabbits were everywhere in the sagebrush on the mesa, and were creating such a nuisance that hunters were encouraged to take pot shots at them. One traveler on a trip from San Diego to Old Town said he counted 135. Favorite spots for hunters of rabbit and quail were in the canyon which became Reynard Way, and on the Peninsula (Coronado and North Island). Hunters found quail plentiful, in fact, two men bagged 35,000 in one winter. Doves were plentiful in Mission Valley, and the deer and antelope played on the plains between Otay and El Cajon. Trout could be found in streams, and the fishing in San Diego bay was excellent. All this served a dual purpose of providing pleasure to the hunters and food for an otherwise limited fare.

The town had a "theatre," Horton's Hall, for local entertainments, and even a few road shows came to town. The Hall boasted three sets of scenery, an indoor set, a marine view, and a woodland set, which provided the appropriate backdrop for the entertainment. Even the circus came to town occasionally. When it did, the whole population trooped up town beyond D to attend. Even during the severest depression, there always seemed to be money for a circus. For years, circuses pitched their tents on the Bancroft Block (B, C, Third and Fourth).

There was a fine baseball field on the Lockling Block (C, D, Sixth & Seventh). This block had been given to L.L. Lockling by Horton in payment for his services in surveying and mapping Horton's Addition. Here, on "Lockling Square," boys and young men organized two teams, the Young Americans and the Golden Eagles. They competed against each other and against a team from Old Town. When important games were played the "uniforms" were their best clothes with "boiled" shirt and starched bosom. There was no such thing as sports clothes in those days, just "old" clothes. To identify the teams, the players wore their insignias "A" or "E" on their cap and shirt.

The Lockling Block remained vacant many years and was used not only as a ball field but as a militia parade ground. When the first building was erected on this block in 1883, the ball games were moved to the block bounded by A, Ash, Third and Fourth.

Horse racing had been a favorite sport at Old Town since the early days. A horse racing track

Fig. 45 J.S. Harbison introduced beekeeping to San Diego County in 1869

was opened in Mission Valley in 1873 with a large crowd in attendance.

The Free Reading Room Association, after it had made its peace with Horton in May, 1873, finally received the gift of his books. On June 6 the association passed a resolution giving grateful acknowledgement to Horton for the valuable library donated to them. The association maintained a room on the west side of Fifth, south of F, next to the Post Office. It was open from 10:00 a.m. to 10:00 p.m. every day. There was only a caretaker in charge, no librarian. The books and magazines were not checked out or indexed, or kept in any particular state of order. As a result, many disappeared. Local residents continued to donate books and the ladies put on many socials and sales, the proceeds going to help maintain the reading room which remained entirely dependent on donations.

San Diego was not without musical talent, or at least had plenty of sympathetic listeners. In 1872 the San Diego Philharmonic Society was organized. A "Grand Concert" was given at Horton's Hall on September 20. The *San Diego Union* reporter, certainly not a "critic" wrote "Undoubtedly the best musical performance ever presented to the citizens of this town." And they didn't even have to go out of town for their musicians.

Those San Diegans fortunate to have a horse and carriage, or able to rent one, enjoyed Sunday drives and picnics at the Old Mission, La Jolla and the Lighthouse on Point Loma, in Rose Canyon and the Sweetwater Valley. The chief means of getting from one place to another within the town was by foot. Walking had not become a lost art, and a stroll in the evening and on Sunday was not only socially acceptable, but the thing to do. The *Union*, on December 28, 1873, told its readers:

"One can have no realizing sense of the special charms of San Diego who has not enjoyed the magnificent view afforded by a stroll over the mesa above the business part of the city. A very short walk up the slope on Sixth Street, just above the beautifully situated residence of Mr. Horton, affords a standpoint whence can be obtained a seaside view that is unsurpassed on the whole coast of California . . . We expect within the next three years to see that whole slope covered with elegant houses as far back as the eye can reach."

The "standpoint" referred to no doubt was at Sixth and Date, the location of Marston Point, which still provides visitors with a breathtaking view of the city.

The temperance movement which had been going strong in the East reached San Diego in the late seventies. In July 1878, local temperance leaders organized a "Band of Hope" in an effort to attract the young people. Its purpose was to instill in its members a "high regard for temperance" (meaning absolute abstention). A badge, in the form of a shield, was given to each member who wore it proudly. The first meeting was held at Horton's Hall and the speaker, inexplicably, was none other than Wallace Leach, a prominent lawyer not noted for his abstinence. Perhaps it was thought he could best describe the effects of "demon rum."

Because the "Band of Hope" engendered enthusiasm among the young fry, soon there was a "Band of Mercy," also furnishing members with a badge in the form of a star. Its lofty purpose was to encourage kindness toward "dumb animals."

During these years Horton was having his ups and downs. He reached his peak, in influence and wealth, in 1873. By the end of that year, his enterprises included: the Horton House, built at a cost of $150,000; his first residence at Tenth and G, later sold to Thomas L. Nesmith, $9000; Horton's Hall, $10,000; his wharf, recently sold to Pacific Mail Steamship Company, $45,000; a "bank" building at Third and D, completed in November 1873 at a cost of $50,000; his residence at Sixth and A, $4500; the Express Building, Sixth and G, $8000; a residence at Ninth and H (occupied by his parents) $1500, and numerous other small buildings.

The collapse of the Scott Boom left him in serious financial difficulty. He had overextended himself, confident that the boom was only the beginning of even better things to come. Only the year before he had been talking of adding sixty rooms to the Horton House. Now he was forced to mortgage it. In February, 1874, he leased it for five years to S.W. Craigue, a wholesale liquor dealer. Three years later Craigue surrendered his lease and Horton again took over control, naming T.A. Judd as the new manager. In October, 1877, Horton leased the hotel to a J.A. Babe, presumably a relation of Mrs. Horton's. In April, 1878, the lease was terminated "by consent" and Horton was again in control. On April 6, 1878, the *Union* reported, "Last evening the Harmony Band serenaded Mr. A.E. Horton at the Horton House as a mark of respect for him as the pioneer of the place, upon his assuming the management of the hotel—the most popular hotel outside of San Francisco. It is needless to say the music was very fine, for the Harmony Band never fails in this regard."

Horton then leased to Chas. P. Gerichten, who was advertising in 1879, "The Horton House, Deutsches Gasthaus of San Diego, 110 Rooms, all light and airy. Day $1.50 to $2.00; Week $8.00 to $14.00; Board per week $7.00; meals 50¢. The bath rooms will always be in readiness with hot and cold water and every other requirement in the best manner."

The Horton House continued to be advertised as First Class and the "Best known hotel south of San Francisco." It became "home" for many winter guests from the East who came to San Diego to get away from the winter snow. The hotel had been the symbol of Horton's success and his greatest pride. He first offered the hotel for sale in 1874 "on advantageous terms." But he could not find a buyer. So, he continued to lease it and struggled to keep up the mortgage payments. It finally proved too much, and in 1881 the mortgage was foreclosed.

Horton remained active in the real estate business, buying and selling, although not on such a grand scale as in the early years. His office now was in his new building, known as the Horton Bank Block, at the southwest corner of Third and D. It was referred to as a bank building, as Horton had expected to lease it to the Bank of San Diego or to the Commercial Bank. There is no record, however, that this building was ever occupied by a bank.

During 1874 lots dropped in price to twenty and thirty dollars, almost to 1867 prices—and 269 parcels, including some of Horton's, were sold for delinquent taxes. There were a few bright spots. In April, 1874, Horton sold $22,000 worth of lots in one day to an Eastern visitor. In May he bought from S.P. Abell a brick building at the northeast corner of Fifth and D, and sold Abell his residence at Sixth and A. It was about this time Horton built a new home for himself, on the northeast corner of First and Elm, at the top of the hill where he liked to go and look over "his" town. It was a small house, a duplicate of the one at Tenth and G. He was determined to push new building north on the mesa, and was confident that if he took the lead others would follow his example.

Horton continued to travel frequently to San Francisco on business. In May, 1874, while there, he met again with General Rosecrans who was confident Col. Scott would get the necessary congressional backing to go ahead with his original plans for the Texas & Pacific. When Horton reported this on his return it offered a glimmer of hope to San

Fig. 46   Horton's Wharf, foot of Fifth Street as it appeared in the 1880s

Fig. 47   The San Diego Harmony
Cornet Band

Diegans. Again, in June, Horton went to San Francisco, still with the interests of San Diego first in mind. This time he went to see Cyrus W. Field. He presented to Field the coast survey charts of San Diego harbor and explained the interest San Diego had in Field's Pacific Cable project. Field told Horton that San Diego's chances were good to be the American terminus of the cable and were probably ahead of any other harbor on the coast. He explained that no commitments could be made until the survey was completed. Field further added that he was sorry for not having time to go to San Diego to inspect the harbor himself, but he had to return East. Here again San Diego would lose out because it did not have as much money or influence as the North. But it was a good try on the part of Horton.

Horton was a familiar passenger on the steamers between San Diego and San Francisco. He would be pointed out to strangers as the founder of the city of San Diego, and a man of wealth and influence. On one of his trips down from San Francisco he struck up a conversation with a stranger who obviously was not aware of Horton's identity. The young man was described as a "dandy" and a typical "lady's man." He asked Horton where he was going. Horton told him he was going to San Diego which he had heard was an up and coming place, and perhaps he would buy some land there. The young man warned him to look out for a man by the name of Horton who was a sharp dealer in real estate, and who was very rich. The stranger then proceeded to inform him that Horton had a daughter and he was going to San Diego to court her, and then gave Horton a knowing wink. Horton

thanked him for the information and said good day. The young man later learned to whom he had been talking. He was not seen in San Diego and must have taken the first conveyance out of town. Horton of course had no daughter, but he did have a niece living with him of whom the stranger must have heard and assumed was his daughter.

Horton was now a church member. In June of 1873 he and Mrs. Horton were among the founders of the Unitarian Society which first met on June 22 at Horton's Hall. The first secretary of that society was Mrs. Lydia M. Knapp, who would in 1890 become the next and last Mrs. Horton. Horton attended fairly regularly, and was known to put a five dollar gold piece in the collection plate if he approved of the sermon. We can assume that if he were present, and no five dollar gold piece was found in the plate, the minister knew his sermon had failed to hit its mark.

Horton had provided well for his parents during their last years. His mother passed away on March 5, 1873, at the age of eighty-five and his father on February 19, 1875, aged eighty-seven. They were both buried in Mt. Hope Cemetery in the Horton family plot.

In September, 1875, Horton advertised 500 lots for sale in Horton's Addition at $100 to $1000 on terms of one fourth down, monthly payments of ten to twenty-five dollars. It is probable that not all these lots were his, but that he was acting as agent for others as well. In November he sold the Abell Building at Fifth and D for $5000 to Governor R.C. McCormick of Arizona.

In 1876 Horton went East, again to see Col.

Scott and to push the interests of San Diego in securing a direct railroad line from the East. On August 10, 1876, Douglas Gunn, editor of the *San Diego Union*, received the following wire:

"Col. Scott says: You may telegraph that we will begin work at San Diego this fall for good.
A.E. Horton"

Another crumb thrown to San Diegans. While in the East, Horton attended the Centennial Celebration in Philadelphia and returned to San Diego on September 15.

On March 15, 1877, Horton's loyal assistant, Jesse Aland Shepherd, passed away at the age of fifty from pneumonia. In the death notices he was lauded as "one of the cornerstones of our young city. He was full of public spirit, and an active, earnest and untiring worker for the common welfare. A more unselfish man never lived...His memory should ever be held in grateful remembrance by the people of San Diego."

In July, 1877, Horton purchased 2500 acres from the Argüello Estate at a delinquent tax sale for $1357.98. This land is bounded on the west by Boundary Street, on the east by Euclid, on the north by Juniper and on the south by National City. The value now would be astronomical, but Horton disposed of all of it, or lost it for delinquent taxes, within a few years.

There was a steady but slow growth of population during the late seventies. The population which had dropped to 1500 rose to about 2000. People were still coming, and remaining, because of the climate, reputed to the the most "equable" in the world and conducive to health and longevity. Doctors in the East and Middle West were advising their patients who had weak lungs or "consumption" to go to Southern California. Many came believing they had only a short time to live and instead became hale and hearty and lived to a ripe old age.

In January, 1879, the Commercial Bank of San Diego brought a foreclosure suit against Sarah W.B. Horton and A.E. Horton and posted a notice of Sheriff's Sale of Block Twelve of Horton's Addition.

It is known that Horton was in financial difficulties, and it was reported that he had turned over all his assets to creditors. This Horton vehemently denied. In spite of his troubles, Horton kept a cheerful outlook. He never once doubted but that everything would turn out all right, and that soon he would be back on "Easy Street." Just as soon as the railroad got to San Diego.

Fig. 48 The San Diego Union building, Sixth and F Streets, in the 1870s

Chapter Nine

At Last, a Railroad! 1880–85

After "Black Friday" and the failure of the Texas & Pacific to complete a railroad to the West coast, the Southern Pacific began buying up Texas and Pacific stock and land. In San Diego law suits were commenced against Scott and the Texas & Pacific to recover the cash and land given as a subsidy, estimated at a value of five million dollars. Eventually the suits were settled, with San Diego accepting back half of the lands, and the Texas & Pacific keeping the other half and all the cash. Obviously, the loss to the city was great.

During the years 1874 and 1875 the Southern Pacific was extending its line south from San Francisco to Los Angeles. When its plans became known, promoters got busy acquiring land along

Fig. 49   First National Bank Building, Fifth and E Streets, about 1883

the proposed route, setting out "paper towns" and then making strenuous efforts to "colonize" them. Many towns sprang up along the proposed route. Some became railroad stops and then grew to sizable communities. Those that were not so fortunate as to be in the path of the railroad soon disappeared and the investment was lost. The towns favored by a railroad depot were mainly those which offered a subsidy to the Southern Pacific. On September 5, 1876, Charles Crocker drove in the golden spike connecting Los Angeles with San Francisco. Los Angeles, the rival to the north, now had its railroad. San Diego was still isolated and ignored.

San Diegans were discouraged, but still determined not to give up their efforts. After all, they reasoned, they were more interested in becoming a western terminus of a line from the East, than in a railroad connection to San Francisco. San Diegans could still get to San Francisco conveniently by boat. They were hopeful, of course, that the Southern Pacific would extend its line from Los Angeles to San Diego. They were even more hopeful that a road could be built east from San Diego. Collis P. Huntington, of the Southern Pacific, came to San Diego and was entertained at the Horton House. But, he let it be understood that he did not think that a route to the east was feasible because part of the tracks would have to go through Mexico.

By 1879 San Diegans still believed their best hope lay with the Texas & Pacific. The San Diego Railroad Committee then appointed Frank Kimball to go to Philadelphia, headquarters of the Texas & Pacific. Col. Scott was no longer president. The strain had taken its toll, his health was failing and he would die in 1881, a broken and discouraged man. While in Philadelphia, Kimball became convinced there was no chance there and so went on to Boston to contact the president of Atchison,

Fig. 50 California Southern Engine
Number Three at the foot of
Fourth Avenue

Topeka & Santa Fe. Kimball offered the Santa Fe large donations of his and his brother's lands if they would establish a terminal at National City. As a result, Santa Fe did express an interest and sent surveyors to San Diego.

The San Diego committee was now satisfied that the Santa Fe offered the best hope, and in the latter part of 1879 offered to turn over to it the lands previously given to the Texas & Pacific. They were sure that it was only a matter of time... But, several months passed and nothing more was heard. Then it was learned the Texas & Pacific had merged with the Santa Fe and their plans had changed.

In May 1880, Kimball was again sent east to Boston. While there he received desperate letters from San Diego. E.W. Morse wrote "The people are leaving every day and soon all will be gone who can get away." And from Rufus Choate, "If you do not succeed in getting a railroad, in less than one year not 500 people will be in the city of San Diego."

Kimball even had a conference with the officials of the Atlantic & Pacific, but with no success. It was apparent to Kimball, and to the committee in San Diego, that powerful northern interests were working against San Diego and were determined to thwart its every effort, no matter what. But Kimball's tenacity paid off. Finally in July, 1880, as a result of his untiring efforts, five officers of Santa Fe agreed to form a syndicate to accept subsidies from San Diego and National City. They incorporated under the name of The San Diego Land & Town Company. Kimball and the committee were jubilant! They arranged to transfer to the new company the land previously given to Scott, together with other donations of land. The Kimballs agreed to transfer most of National City. In October the proposed railroad was incorporated under the name of The California Southern Railroad.

It appeared that at last San Diego would have a

65

railroad. The *Union* on December 26, 1880, reported that "Christmas Day dawned on the people of San Diego in a season of prosperity—with a brighter promise of the future than they have had for many years." The proposed route for the California Southern was from National City, by way of San Diego, Encinitas, Temecula, and San Jacinto, to Colton. At Colton it would cross the tracks of the Southern Pacific to join the Atlantic & Pacific at Waterman Junction (Barstow).

Work commenced in National City. A roundhouse, wharfs and yards were built. The work was slow, with many delays due to incompetent and inexperienced help, resulting in additional costs. On July 11, 1881, the brig *Orient* brought to National City the first locomotive, but it was of the largest type made, and completely unsuitable for the winding track of the California Southern. On July 27, 1881, the first train left from National City for San Diego. There would be two stations in San Diego, one at the foot of Twenty-Second Street, and the other at the foot of D.

By September, the tracks had been laid as far as False Bay on a route through Old Town. In surveying the route through Temecula, the tracks were to go along the creek bed. The surveyors were warned by old residents there would be a danger of flood and they should lay the tracks higher on the hillside. But the surveyors were unimpressed and ignored these warnings.

By August of 1882, 182 miles of track had been laid to Colton, but there the work had to stop. The Southern Pacific would not allow California Southern to cross its tracks. A law suit resulted, which was finally resolved in favor of California Southern. But in the meantime, passengers had a two hour stage ride from Colton to connect with the Atlantic & Pacific.

By September, 1883, the tracks, now permitted to cross at Colton, reached San Bernardino. In January San Diegans learned the syndicate controlling the California Southern was dickering to sell the line to the Santa Fe. This was not surprising because almost all of the directors were also Santa Fe officials. Then, on February 28, 1884, Southern California suffered a twenty inch downpour and thirty miles of roadbed from San Luis Rey (Oceanside) to Temecula were washed out. The flood came so fast a train had to be abandoned at Santa Margarita Ranch and the passengers forced to get to safety through mud and water the best they could. The old timers' warnings were proved right, but by then it was too late. Again, in order to get out of San Diego, travelers were obliged to go by boat or stage. Repairs were commenced, the line was rerouted along the coast, and the tracks from San Bernardino to Waterman Junction were completed. Waterman Junction was named for Governor Robert Waterman who had large silver mine holdings there. Its name was changed to Barstow in 1886.

Finally, on November 9, 1885, the last spike was driven in at Cajon Pass connecting the California Southern with the Atchison Topeka & Santa Fe at Waterman Junction. The first train from San Diego to the east left the little wooden depot at the foot of D on November 15. San Diego and National City were ready to celebrate, and celebrate they did—for two days. San Diego held its festivities on the eighteenth, and National City on the nineteenth. The two Founding Fathers, Horton and Kimball, were on hand, each praising the other. Any past jealousy or rivalry seemed to be forgotten. Horton was chairman of the San Diego celebration, and in a little speech he gave full credit to Kimball for his great accomplishment. Then, on November 21 the first through train from the east arrived, in a driving rain, but with all the city officals and many residents huddled under umbrellas waiting to greet the sixty arriving passengers. The train consisted of two coaches, a mail and baggage car. A brass band was on hand and in spite of the weather, fireworks were shot into the sky with noise and a spectacular display. San Diego had its railroad to the East. The Atlantic Coast was now only a week away!

The "Boom of the Eighties" in San Diego generally dates from the completion of the California Southern. But in the early eighties, with the promise of a railroad becoming a reality, business picked up and there was a spurt in population. Those who wanted to be in at the start and take advantage of the crowds that were sure to come, began investing in real estate and starting new businesses. The population of the city in 1870 was 2300. By 1880 it had grown only to 2637, but after 1880 it grew rapidly to a peak of around 40,000 in 1887. This meant that more hotels would be needed.

In 1883, W.W. Bowers announced he had acquired the block bounded by Third, Fourth, Fir and Grape, and would build a luxurious hotel on the site. True, this was way up on the hill, far from the center of town, with only a rough dirt road leading to it. It had previously been the site of Indian huts, and sheep still grazed in the vicinity. It was two blocks east of the residence Horton built for himself at First and Elm. Just as Horton had built the Horton House way out north of the city, four-

Fig. 51 The Florence Hotel, Fourth
and Fir Streets

teen years later Bowers would do the same with his hotel.

The new hotel opened on February 24, 1884, with a gala ball and became the show place of the city during the boom days. It was called The Villa, or The Florence, and the surrounding area became known as Florence Heights. An advertisement of 1886 described the Florence Hotel thus:

Situated on the high mesa lands, overlooking the entire city and bay, and the magnificent Coronado Beach, is the Villa Hotel, owned and conducted by W.W. Bowers. It occupies an entire block of land bounded by Third, Fourth, Fir and Grape Streets. The hotel structure itself is large and commodious, and most elegantly arranged; the remainder of the block, after reserving large and beautifully arranged grounds, is occupied by separate, tastily built and beautifully furnished cottages for the use of those who prefer the similitude of a home rather than the more public hotel building proper. The Florence is not only strictly first class, but it is really the most exclusive, and the most tony hotel in the city; and yet it is most delightfully free from that painful stiffness and unpleasant "shoddy-aristocracy" air which pervade many such places.

The hotel was also described as being eight blocks from the business center of the city, with a carriage provided to the center of town and return every thirty minutes. It faced south on Fir Street and had a wide panoramic view over the growing city. Its gardens and grounds were especially beautiful. The Florence in later years became the Casa Loma and then was torn down, leaving on the site only a rare Moreton Bay fig tree, which, in spite of neglect, still fights for its life.

In 1885 San Diego acquired its first skyscraper, the Santa Rosa, later the St. James Hotel, on F Street, between Sixth and Seventh. The site is now occupied by the Maryland Hotel. The Santa Rosa was built by Dr. P.C. Remondino, a native of Italy, who had served in the Union Army and established an active medical practice in San Diego. He was City Physician in 1875-76, and in 1881, with Dr. Thomas C. Stockton, established a sanitarium at

Columbia and F in one of the old buildings formerly used by the barracks. The new hotel was an unbelievable five stories. It had a mansard roof, lots of gingerbread decorations, and the top floors were covered with round tin plates that reflected in the sun and glittered like mirrors. The tin decorations caused United States Senator George Hearst, a distinguished guest, to exclaim, "Magnificent! Where is your tin mine?" The hotel boasted 150 rooms. Its bar on F Street became the place where local business tycoons liked to transact their business. During the height of the boom in 1887 an annex was built at Seventh and F. During its heyday many prominent guests stopped there, including Governor Waterman, Joaquin Miller and Lily Langtry. With the collapse of the boom it became a rooming house, and the Post Office which had been across the street at the corner of Sixth and F, moved to the Annex. The building was demolished in 1912.

In April, 1881, the San Diego Gas & Oil Company was organized. It built its plant on the block bounded by Ninth, Tenth, M and N. Petroleum was the fuel used at first, but in 1883 it was changed to coal. Gas mains were laid and on the night of June 4, 1881 a few street lights were turned on for the first time. The whole town turned out to admire the spectacle. The first subscribers to this new luxury numbered eighty-nine out of a population of around 3000.

In May, 1882, the San Diego Telephone Company was organized. The first use of the telephone

Fig. 52 St. James Hotel

was on June 11 with thirteen subscribers, mostly businesses. This new invention was accepted readily and by 1887 the company could boast 284 subscribers.

For several years, San Diego's only bank had been the Consolidated Bank of San Diego at Fifth and G—a consolidation of the Bank of San Diego and the Commercial Bank. In June, 1883, the Bank of Southern California was formed with Jacob Gruendike as president. It was located in a one story building at the northwest corner of Fifth and E. In 1885 its name was changed to First National Bank.

In the mid eighties the products produced and shipped out of San Diego in greatest volume were wheat, wool and honey, in that order. San Diego County became known as the "Honey Capitol." In 1885, 2,679,747 pounds of honey were produced, with two million pounds exported. Fruit growing was expanding in National City and in the Sweetwater and Tijuana valleys. Truck gardens were beginning to dot Mission Valley.

Stock raising, formerly the first industry in California, was a dwindling occupation, although San Diego was the last county to abandon it as a leading industry. From 1868 on the town grew faster than the interior regions because it was thought "nothing would grow here." Experimentation, especially in National City, proved otherwise. Soon Rancho de la Nación was producing apples, grapes, raisins, peaches, pears, figs, apricots, berries, olives, in addition to citrus fruit. In September 1880 the first County Fair was held at National City and showed the capacity for fruit growing in the area. It was said the displays of fruit, both in variety and quality, were unsurpassed in any fruit growing community in the world. Visitors to the fair, even local residents, were amazed!

With the production of these commodities came the need to transport them to a market. A railroad was a necessity. Before the railroad was completed, these shipments had to go to Los Angeles or San Francisco by boat and then east, resulting in delays and spoilage. With a direct line to the east, completed in 1885, large quantities of honey, oranges, lemons, potatoes, salt, fish, butter and wool could be shipped across country in a matter of a week's time.

With the growth of population, San Diego was now becoming more club and lodge minded. It already had a Masonic Lodge. The first Masonic Lodge in Southern California was organized November 20, 1851 at Old Town. It moved to New Town in 1870. In 1888 the Eastern Star was organized and the Silvergate Lodge in 1889. The Masonic Hall, built in the eighties, was an impressive building at Sixth and H. An Odd Fellows Lodge had been in existence since 1868. In 1881 members of the G.A.R. organized Heintzelman Post #33, indicating that the Copperheads had given way to the Northerners!

On March 17, 1882, the first meeting of the Y.M.C.A. was held in the store of George W. Marston, at Fifth and F. Marston was named its first president. Its meetings were thereafter held in Hubbell's Hall, next to Marston's store, and then at the Masonic Hall. The Y.W.C.A. came into being in September, 1886 with twenty members. It met once a month at Keener Chapel, Seventh and D.

On May 19, 1882, again with George W. Marston spearheading the action, the San Diego Free Public Library was organized, succeeding the old Reading Room. Now the city would partially support it, although cash donations and gifts of books were requested and gratefully accepted. The library opened on July 12 in rooms donated by the Consolidated Bank on its second floor, with Archibald Hooker as librarian. He also doubled as janitor.

In 1884 Frances Willard arrived in San Diego, the first of the vanguard of temperance believers. When she left, San Diego had an official Women's Christian Temperance Union. This society was so active and zealous in its money raising projects for their "cause" that by 1887 it had $1000 in its treasury. With this money they acquired a house at 1365 Sixteenth Street as a "home for indigent gentlewomen." Not, it will be noted, a home for reformed alcoholics. This house and property would later become the site of the San Diego Children's Home.

Frances Willard must have found Southern California a fertile field for her endeavors. Even with droughts and lack of water no one needed to go far for liquid refreshment. There was always a saloon handy for any emergency. The women of San Diego, living in a closely knit community, were aware of the problem but were helpless to know what to do. They had no vote or political influence and so the W.C.T.U. offered them a "cause" they could wholeheartedly support.

There were no organized charities. People were expected to help their relatives. Occasionally a collection would be taken for a needy person or family. If they wanted to leave San Diego to join their families elsewhere or look for work, the steamships were cooperative and would assist. After the Indians left for their reservations the Mexicans

Fig. 53   Horton's Mansion, built in
1885 on First, between Fir
and Grape Streets

were the most destitute. It was in 1883 that Helen Hunt Jackson came to San Diego to gather material for her book *Ramona*, published in 1885. The novel called to the attention of the world the plight of the Indians, just as Harriet Beecher Stowe's *Uncle Tom's Cabin* had done earlier for the blacks. Mrs. Jackson visited Indian reservations in San Diego and Riverside and made many friends. One of her confidants was Father Ubach, who ever afterward was known as "Father Gaspara" in the story, *Ramona*.

In 1880 the county acquired a farm in Mission Valley, near the foot of Sixth Street and established a County Farm where needy could live and work. It became known as the Poor Farm and the road leading down the hill was Poor Farm Road. The first County Hospital was built on this site, later moving to the top of the hill in Hillcrest, in 1903.

In spite of San Diego's growth, nothing much was done about the city streets, still dust-filled when dry, and muddy when the rains came. As early as 1869 a proposal had been made to license saloons and teamsters for the purpose of raising funds for street improvements, but this was voted down. In October, 1872, the city engineer was instructed to make a survey for grading the streets from A Street south, and from Thirteenth Street west, to the bay. Fifth Street was the first to be graded, and in 1880 it was extended out on the mesa. Sheep grazing on the mesa ceased during the eighties as roads and building pushed north. The center of town was moving north. F Street was now thought to become the main artery cross town, and a flurry of building started along that street west and east of Fifth Street. Down at the barracks the infantry used H Street for target practice. This went on until the traffic to Coronado began. Every night at the barracks a cannon was fired. This continued until the nineties, in spite of many complaints that the noise frightened the horses.

During the eighties Horton's influence began to wane. He was acknowledged "Father" of San Diego, but with the loss of money went much of his power and influence. Other men of wealth were beginning to be attracted to San Diego for investment in its future growth. In May, 1880, Horton announced his candidacy for city trustee in the Fourth Ward. Again he was defeated. Of the 119 votes cast, Horton received fifty-five, but sixty-four were cast for his opponent, John H. Snyder. This was his last attempt at political office.

In July, 1881, the Hortons, with Mr. and Mrs. Morse and Mrs. Fidelia Shepherd, went on a camping trip to Temecula along the road being surveyed for the railroad. They camped at a hot mineral springs in a beautiful canyon five miles from the railroad route. When they returned Horton was enthusiastic. He said bathing in the hot springs had made a new man of him. His hearing had been bothering him but after a few days of taking these waters he was completely cured. He praised these springs as a "Fountain of Youth" and superior to the Indian springs at Warner's Ranch. He prophesied the location would become a great resort. These springs later became known as Murrieta Hot Springs.

Horton was still active in the real estate business, dealing mostly in his own properties. During the mid-eighties his fortunes picked up along with the rest of San Diego in the vanguard of the railroad boom. By 1885 he was at last able to make another of his dreams come true. He would now build the hilltop mansion he had promised himself. As long ago as 1872 he had announced plans for the most elegant house in Southern California to be built at a cost of $25,000 on the block bounded by First, Second, Fir and Grape. Then came the depression after the Scott Boom and he settled for a home at Sixth and A. In the mid seventies financial problems kept him from building his mansion but he did build a more modest home on the northeast corner of First and Elm.

Horton's mansion at 1929 First Street, in the middle of the block, between Fir and Grape, was finally completed in 1885. It contained twelve large rooms. The woodwork was of rare, curly redwood. The fireplaces were works of art, several being of black inlaid marble. Again workmen came from San Francisco, and many were paid in lots, of which Horton had more than cash. Nothing was too fine either for the building or its furnishings. The landscaping was elaborate and formal with much marble statuary. The grounds were terraced down to the street, with a retaining wall at the bottom. Guarding the gate, at the foot of the stairs leading up to the house, were two gilded and life sized iron lion heads. On the roof of the two story building was a lookout and widow's walk where Horton could watch through his spyglass for ships rounding Point Loma. He would run up a flag signalling his neighbors of the approaching ship and then would hurry in his carriage to the steamship wharf to be on hand to greet the newcomers.

The cost of the new house was probably closer to $18,000 than $25,000. However, there was no question but that it had a "million dollar" view and it certainly was the most elegant house in San Diego, if not in Southern California. The big white house on the hill was an attraction for visitors and local residents who all agreed it was a fitting home for the Founder of San Diego.

CALIFORNIA SOUTHERN
RAILROAD COMPANY.

All rail line between National City, San Diego and Los Angeles, and points East and West. Close connection at Barstow with A. & P. R. R., and at Los Angeles with S. P. R. R.

(Pullman Sleeping Cars on Passenger Trains.
Through tickets to eastern points, and to and from Europe, with choice of routes.
Time Table Taking Effect Sunday, June 20 1886.

Fig. 54 Notice in the *San Diego Union,* 1886, for the California Southern advertised "Close connection" and "Pullman Sleeping Cars"

Chapter Ten

The Big Boom, 1886–88

The trickle of newcomers that began with the promise of a railroad in 1880 gained momentum each year and became a flood in 1886. The population, which in 1885 was around 5000, reached 35,000 by 1887 and rose to a peak of 40,000 at the height of the boom in early 1888. It was impossible to build hotels and houses fast enough to accommodate the thousands who were now arriving each month with all their household goods by rail, boat, stagecoach and wagon. On the block bounded by Eighth, Ninth, I and J, was Granger's Corral, a camp with cooking facilities for the wagons arriving from the north. The new settlers were allowed to sleep in their wagons, or under them, until other accommodations could be found. The San Diego Tent & Awning Company, on Fourth between E and F, did a big business in providing temporary tent houses.

In 1886 arrivals by rail were estimated at between 2000 and 3000 a month. This rose to 3000 to 5000 a month in 1887, until they reached a peak of more than 5000 during the months of July to September, 1887. A new Grand Union Depot was built at the foot of D, replacing the little wooden Santa Fe station.

In addition, there were over 1000 ship arrivals in 1887, each crowded with passengers for San Diego and its neighboring "boom towns." Ships were gaily welcomed, with large crowds waiting at the dock to greet the newcomers. Word was reaching the East Coast that Southern California was a veritable paradise, with a perfect climate, neither too hot nor too cold, just right. Those who had already arrived, wrote home glowingly about how cheaply one could live here, only a few acres would support a family. There was no snow to shovel and no need to worry about heat for the house. Today's residents, with their heated and air conditioned homes, have to admit those early residents must have been hardy souls.

Now the railroads were advertising in a big way for passengers. The one-way fare from St. Louis to Los Angeles had been as much as $150. Then rates began to drop as competition became more keen. Soon there was a rate war between the Southern Pacific and Santa Fe. Fares went down to $100, then to $75, and on down and down until in March of 1887 it was actually possible to go from Chicago to Los Angeles for $1.00! For almost a year the rates were not over $25. The railroads with their excursion fares kept putting on more and more trains. Whole communities traveled together on emigrant trains. Quakers came to Whittier, Germans to Olivenhain and Anaheim. By 1887 three to five excursion trains were arriving each day in California. With fares so low and with such glowing reports of what was at the end of the line, why should not hundreds and thousands of Midwesterners and Easterners go out on a one-way ticket to see for themselves. Only a few ever inquired about the price of a return ticket.

There was no question about it, San Diego was booming. And as it was during the Scott Boom, residents could not believe it was just temporary. They were sure it would go on forever, and now, at last, San Diego would become a great city, perhaps the largest in California. The climate rush was on, and it was worth more to Southern California than a gold rush. In 1886 T.S. Van Dyke wrote about the growing hordes, "It was plain that they were in fact buying comfort, immunity from snow and slush, from piercing winds and sleet clad streets, from sultry days and sleepless nights, from thunderstorms, cyclones, malaria, mosquitoes and bedbugs." There was some question in San Diego about the latter two.

In 1886 the suspicions of San Diegans were proven correct when the Santa Fe took over control of the California Southern, but they were not prepared for what was to come. First, the superintendent's office, which had been in National City, was moved to San Diego. Then the repair shops, promised for National City and San Diego, were set up at Colton and San Bernardino. In March, 1887, the superintendent moved to Los Angeles and the shops to San Bernardino. There was an exodus from San Diego of railroad workers. This was a blow to San Diegans and all they had worked for, but for awhile it was cushioned by the continued influx of people.

San Diego's boom was helped along and given great impetus by the arrival of two Easterners of influence and wealth, Elisha S. Babcock, a railroad man from Indiana, and H. L. Story, a piano manufacturer from Chicago. They came West in 1884 for their health, which they promptly regained, and began to look around for possible investment opportunities. They liked to row across the bay to

hunt rabbits on San Diego's peninsula. On one of their visits, they hit on the idea that here was the perfect spot for a luxury hotel. Soon they formed a syndicate bringing in with them E.S. Babcock, Jr., Jacob Gruendike, the San Diego banker, General H.W. Halleck and Frederick Billings. In April, 1886, they incorporated under the name of the Coronado Beach Company, giving the peninsula its new name. They had purchased the entire peninsula for $110,000 in December, 1885. Soon the Coronado Beach Company was in business with offices at Fifth and E in the same building as

Fig. 55 Bird's Eye View of the proposed community of Coronado Beach

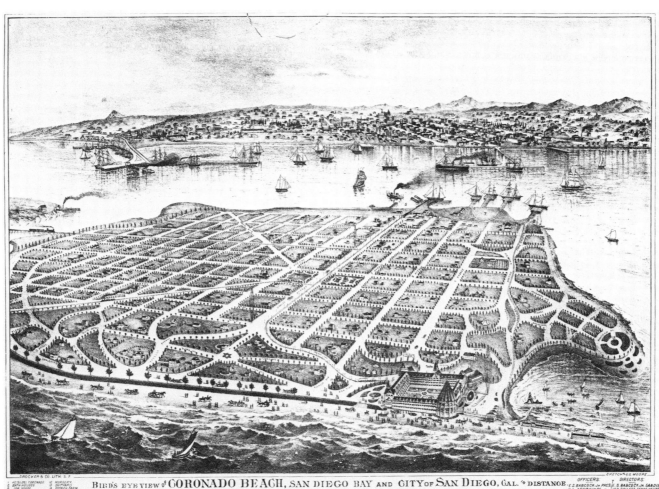

BIRD'S EYE VIEW of CORONADO BEACH, SAN DIEGO BAY AND CITY of SAN DIEGO, CAL. DISTANCE.

CORONADO BEACH COMPANY.

CAPITAL—ONE MILLION DOLLARS.

Fig. 56   A detailed lithograph
depicts a booming San
Diego, looking across the
bay to Coronado and Point
Loma

the First National Bank. They promised to build
"the largest hotel in the world" and one "too
gorgeous to be true." The land was surveyed, with
lots and blocks set out, and on November 13,
1886, the first auction of lots was held. Six thousand persons attended, and a million dollars worth
of lots were sold in a short time, far more than the
promoters had even dared dream. On the proposed
site for the hotel, a pavilion was built where visitors
could stand and admire the superb view of Mexico,
Point Loma and the neighboring Coronado Islands,
from which the peninsula took its new name.

Coronado, except for the hotel, was to be strictly
"dry." Every deed carried a restriction that no
spirituous liquors could be manufactured or sold
on the premises. In spite of objections, the seller
remained firm, the hotel would have a complete
monopoly on the drinks. Even so, this seemed to
have no detrimental effect on the sale of lots. By
January, 1887, Coronado could boast of thirty
dwellings, and in March actual construction began
on the hotel.

To Babcock and Story also goes the credit for
the first local public transportation in San Diego. It
was Babcock who ordered the first ferry boat to ply
from the foot of H, to Coronado. The San Diego
and Coronado Ferry Company was organized in
1886. Babcock and Story then built a wharf at the
foot of H, almost on the exact spot of the old Davis
wharf, as well as a ferry wharf. All material and supplies used in construction of the hotel were
brought in to this wharf and then ferried across to

Coronado. A railroad, the Coronado Belt Line, was built to go from the Fifth Street wharf around the bay and strand to the ferry landing at Coronado, a distance of 21.29 miles.

Also in 1886, Babcock and Story organized the San Diego Street Car Company. A mule car was provided from the ferry landing to D, and then to Fifth Street. The first horse car left the foot of Fifth on July 4, 1886, and went up Fifth as far as the Florence Hotel. Soon a second car left the foot of D, going east one and a quarter miles. A third, on H, went from the wharf east to Sixteenth. These lines were extended rapidly and later became electric. By January of 1888, at the height of the boom, thirty-six miles of streetcar railway was in operation.

Electricity came to San Diego in 1886 when the Jenney Electric Company of Indianapolis started operations here. Its first customer was the Horton House. It soon constructed six 110 foot electric-carbon arc lamps in the central area. These were

later increased to twenty-four. The arc lamps were turned on for the first time on the evening of March 16, 1886, and operated only until midnight. Until 1902 they were on "moonlight" schedule, shut down when there was a full moon or plenty of moonlight. These lamps stood for more than thirty years, and because they loomed over the buildings, were used as markers by ships coming into the harbor.

In January, 1887, E.S. Babcock and his Coronado Gas & Electric Company bought out the interest of Jenney Electric Company. In May he consolidated it with the San Diego Gas Company to form the San Diego Gas Fuel and Electric Light Company. It generated electricity from its plant at Tenth and M, and then opened a business office for the convenience of customers at 935 Sixth Street. This company furnished gas and light for San Diego and Coronado.

In San Diego real estate prices rose to

Fig. 57 E.S. Babcock, H.L. Story,
A.E. Horton and Nat Titus
at the Pavilion on the site of
the Coronado Hotel, 1886

astronomical heights. Lots that a few months earlier had sold for a few hundred dollars, now were priced in the thousands, only to double or triple again with each successive sale. Lots in the business district which had sold for twenty-five dollars a front foot, now went as high as $2500 a front foot. $40,000 was paid for a corner lot. Lots in Middletown, farther from the center of town, were being advertised for $125. Even land in Mission Valley, considered relatively worthless and suitable only for growing vegetables and alfalfa, was selling for thirty-five dollars to $150 an acre, ridiculously high. Store rentals went to as much as $500 a month. Hotel rates were one to four dollars a night, and those without reservations had to sleep in the lobby. Carpenters and bricklayers, now much in demand, were receiving five to eight dollars a day. Barbers were getting as much as twenty-five cents for a shave, and forty cents for a bath. To rent a horse and buggy cost two dollars and fifty cents an hour.

New homes were mushrooming to the east on Golden Hill, and to the north on the mesa around the Florence Hotel. And there was a frenzy of business building—offices, stores, hotels, banks,

theatres, churches and schools. E.W. Morse and E.R. Pierce built what became known as the Pierce-Morse Block, on the northwest corner of Sixth and F. It was said to be "The first building thoroughly metropolitan in appearance erected in San Diego." Not all of the buildings were slapped together hurriedly. Many were of fine construction, and used only the best of material and workmanship. This is evident by the number of buildings erected in the eighties that are still in use today. Several buildings erected on Fifth and Sixth between H and D are still standing, although greatly remodeled. Some, above the ground floor, appear very much as they did in those days. Two of these buildings are the Nesmith & Greeley Building and the present Ratner Building, both on Fifth between E and F.

In 1886 the Sun Building was erected at 940 Fourth, at the southeast corner of the plaza. This building was also used for offices. It housed some city offices, including the Justice Courts of San Diego Township. The Chamber of Commerce, now boasting sixty-four members, met once a month in that building.

Another newspaper, starting publication in 1887, was the *Deutsche Zeitung*, a German language weekly. San Diego from its very beginning had a large German speaking population, many being recent immigrants who came almost at once from the old country to Southern California. The *Deutsche Zeitung* was published regularly until World War I.

The leader of the German community was

Joseph Winter who established the San Diego Steam Cracker Bakery at Fourth and H. He advertised it as "The largest steam bakery in Southern California." There was a Winter's Bakery in San Diego for many years. There was also a German "Biergarten" on the northwest corner of Fifth and B, owned by Anton Mayrhofer. The gardens extended through to Fourth Street. This Biergarten was a popular meeting place for the more respectable of the community who would not deign to patronize the livelier saloons near the waterfront.

Another large new brick structure was the Bancroft Block, at the southeast corner of Fifth and G. It had four stories and was built at a cost of $40,000. A commercial college occupied the top floor, teaching shorthand, typing, grammar and bookkeeping. A dry goods store, the City of Paris, was on the ground floor.

In 1886, on the site previously occupied by the Episcopal Church at the southeast corner of Fourth and C, a "rococco palace," the Brewster Hotel, was erected. It was designed as a commercial hotel, but was "magnificent in all its appointments." It advertised "Fine large sample rooms for commercial travelers." It was the first building in San Diego to have a passenger elevator. It also offered the luxuries of hot and cold water, gas, and even an elegant drugstore known as the Brewster Pharmacy. This building was used as a hotel until it was razed in 1934.

Until the eighties, Horton's Hall was the only theatre in the town. In 1881 Wallace Leach, a prominent attorney, opened Leach's Athletic Hall, on the north side of D, between First and Second. In 1887 this building was converted to a theatre and given the fancy name of Leach's Opera House. It seated 800, considerably more than Horton's Hall, and was used principally for traveling stock companies. The building was of redwood, fifty feet wide, one hundred feet long, and had a twenty-five foot stage.

Wallace Leach was a colorful character, to say the least. He was a capable attorney, but unfor-

Fig. 58   Joseph Winter's Bakery at
Fourth and H about 1880

Fig. 59 The plaza in the early 1880s

Fig. 60 Temple Beth Israel at
Second and Beech

tunately was a heavy drinker and frequently at odds with the police at whom he liked to take pot shots. Fortunately for the police his marksmanship, especially when drunk, was not too good. On May 13, 1888, Leach was thrown from a horse at First and D and received injuries from which he died. In 1889 Jack Dodge took over Leach's Opera House, and renamed it the D Street Theatre, booking traveling attractions of various kinds.

In 1887 Isadore Louis built the Louis Opera House, on the east side of Fifth between B and C. On May 4 and 5, 1888, Lily Langtry, the "Jersey Lily," appeared there in a drama entitled "A Wife's Peril." This was one of the biggest social events of the year.

The churches were also experiencing a boom, not only in members but in their finances, and were able to construct new buildings. Several new churches came into being, but they were too late to benefit from Horton's offer of free lots.

The Congregationalists organized in September, 1886. The organizers included Mr. and Mrs. George W. Marston and Mr. and Mrs. Myron T. Gilmore. Their first service was held on October 10. The church then leased a building at Ninth and F for ten years. On July 4, 1897, dedication services were held in their beautiful new edifice at Sixth and A.

The Central Christian Church, organized October 27, 1887, first met in Keener Chapel, Seventh and D, on the site of the present Home Tower. In 1901 it moved to the southeast corner of Ninth and F in a small frame building. In 1909 a large church was built on that site.

The Lutherans held their first service on October 21, 1888, in Good Templars' Hall on Third Street. They continued to meet in various locations until they built at 1320 Second Street. Their new building was dedicated April 8, 1894.

Since its early days, San Diego had a sizable Jewish community. In 1872 a Hebrew congregation had been organized in Old Town at the home of Marcus Schiller with eighteen members. In 1888 the Congregation Beth Israel was incorporated and in 1889 its synagogue was built at Second and Beech.

The Seventh Day Adventists organized after an Adventist missionary held evangelistic services in a tent at Sixth and G. In 1888 they erected a church at Eighteenth and G.

On March 31, 1888, at the southeast corner of the plaza, at a spot now marked with a plaque, there was held the first meeting in San Diego of the Salvation Army, an organization formed only a few

Fig. 61 The Pierce-Morse Building, Sixth and F

BOOMING SAN DIEGO!

The metropolis of the New Southwest and the terminus of the overland railroads to Southern California, of the Pacific Coast Steamship company, of the Mexican coast line of steamers, situated on the finest harbor, with one exception, on the Pacific Coast from Central America to Alaska.

Population in 1886.................................	7,500
Population in November 1, 1887.....................	25,000
Value of buildings in course of erection November 1, 1887......	$ 2,000,000
Value of public improvements under way.....................	1,000,000
Extent of Public Park, acres.................................	1,400
Money on deposit at the banks...............................	$ 2,500,000

Fig. 62 Portion of an 1880's real estate ad promotes the rapid growth of San Diego

years before in England. The meeting was marred by rock throwing and general disapproval on the part of local churchgoers. As a result, it had rough going for a few years. In 1889, it established its headquarters on Third between D and E and remained at this site for thirty-nine years.

San Diego, from its earliest days, always had a band ready and eager to perform on the slightest excuse. A City Guard Band was organized in January, 1885, and gave weekly concerts at the bandstand in the plaza. The City Guard met at Armory Hall, on Second, between D and E, in what had been a skating rink. In 1887 the band, while under the direction of "Uncle" Charley Jones, was prevailed upon to make a "Booster Trip" to the East at a cost of $13,000 which was to be raised by popular subscription. Jack Dodge, a cornetist, handled the finances. Twenty-one players, in fancy new uniforms, tooted and pounded their way across the country for forty-two days. Each member was paid on the basis of what he would have earned per day in San Diego. They played at every train stop where they had enough time to get into action. Concerts were given in San Bernardino, Denver, Kansas City, Chicago, St. Louis, Cincinnati, Philadelphia, Niagara Falls, New York City,

Baltimore and even at Harper's Ferry. At the St. Louis Exposition the band was given first place in a G.A.R. National Encampment, being followed by none other than President Grover Cleveland. The Los Angeles band brought up the rear.

The band was always on hand for the Fourth of July celebrations. The Guard's old cannon would be trundled to the plaza and shot off at noon. This did not last too many years, however. The concussion was so great that it rattled windows and broke dishes, causing numerous complaints. After that a Mr. Nottage fired the salute with an anvil until he died in 1891. Noise was a requisite of every celebration. The Fourth of July and other celebrations also brought out a clown division known as "The Horribles," composed of any resident willing to dress to fit the description. Torchlight parades were frequent and long. These would be organized at the throw of a hat, for political, patriotic or any excuse. Fireworks were always available in Chinatown. Chinese New Year was an occasion for more fireworks than the Fourth of July. In addition to the brass bands, cannon and fireworks, there was always an appropriate oration by some distinguished citizen. On July 4, 1888, the speaker of the day at the plaza was a woman, Clara Shortridge Foltz. Mrs. Foltz was a lawyer, admitted in 1878, the first woman to be admitted to practice law in California. In 1888 her residence and office was at the southeast corner of Seventh and F. She was at the same time editor of a daily newspaper, the *Bee*, which in 1889 merged with the *Union*. A few years later, Mrs. Foltz became a Deputy District Attorney in Los Angeles, believed to be the first woman in the United States to hold such a position. In 1930 she ran for governor of California. Her brother, Samuel Shortridge, was more successful politically. He served as United States Senator from California from 1920 until 1933.

In 1887 the Cuyamaca Club was organized as a purely social club. Heber Ingle was the first president. It first met in the Bancroft Building, Fifth and G, and later moved to Sixth and D. In 1908 it moved to the top floor of the new Union Building, where it remained until it moved to the United States National Bank Building.

Both the San Diego Medical Society and the San Diego County Dental Society first saw the light of day in 1887. At that time San Diego had seventy-three physicians and eleven dentists.

The San Diego Rowing Club was organized in 1888 with sixty-one members and five boats. It met at Steadman's Boathouse, foot of F. On Admission Day, September 9, 1888, it held its first gala regatta. It moved in 1897 to the foot of Fifth Street.

Midway along the Fifth Street wharf was Collier's Bathhouse, opened in 1880, which contained a good-sized divided tank for segregation of the sexes. This bathhouse, of course, was intended for swimming. During the eighties there were nine "bathhouses" in San Diego. Most of these were intended for what their name implies. Home bathtubs were not yet in abundant supply, or even considered a household necessity.

Another San Diego social club was The Dashaway Club. It met for "fun and dancing" at Horton's Hall. There were plenty of opportunities for "fun and games" on San Diego's Barbary Coast, better known as the Stingaree District. San Diego was a "wide open" town, in spite of sporadic efforts (not too strenuous) to tone things down when complaints got too numerous. This "entertainment" area was west of Fifth and south of H, although

Fig. 63 The Cuyamaca Club

Third and "I" could be the "heart" of the Stingaree District.

Along with legitimate Chinese laundries, fishermen and vegetable peddlers, were the opium dens, gambling halls and cribs for the "China dolls." Interspersed with legitimate businesses were the "fancy houses" and shacks or cribs, where the girls, painted and crimped, sat at lace curtained windows.

For the bar hopper, or more correctly, the saloon hopper, the most likely place to go was the waterfront. Remember, at that time, the water came up to L Street. At the foot of Fifth was the "Last Chance Saloon." It also advertised "the first chance to get a drink when coming *off* a boat." Another popular saloon at the foot of Fifth was Till Burns' Place. Although one might guess otherwise from the name, Till was a man. Another on the waterfront was the Snug Harbor, offering a schooner of beer for a nickel.

At Third and "I" were a couple of the more rugged spots, the Rosebud and the Silver Moon. The latter finally was closed down because of its refusal, or failure, to pay the city license and taxes. On lower Fourth was the Austrian Beer Hall, where more German was spoken than English. The north side of J between Third and Fourth, and both sides of Third between I and J were lined with gambling houses. A Chinese would be seated in front of each

establishment, holding a string attached to the latch. If a suspicious character (meaning the police) was seen approaching, a pull on the string caused a wooden bar to fall into place, firmly barring the door. This gave those inside time to destroy the evidence and escape through a maze of interlocking rooms before the door could be broken open by the law. Raids on these places were not so much to control the gambling as to look for caches of opium.

During the height of the boom there were sixty-four places where one could buy groceries, but there were seventy-one saloons, most of them located in or around the Stingaree District. Also, at the height of the boom, there were allegedly 120 bawdy houses. In the daytime the "girls" paraded through the streets, often in expensive carriages. Some of the more elite houses even sent out engraved cards inviting gentlemen to their receptions and "high teas."

In 1887 there came on the San Diego scene a man whose name is even more famous today than it was then, Wyatt Earp. Famous for his gun battles in Dodge City and Arizona, Earp came to San Diego from Tombstone. He was listed in the San Diego Directory for 1889 as a "Capitalist." He set up three gambling establishments, one on Sixth next to Hotel St. James, one on E near Sixth and another on Fourth between D and E across from the plaza. Faro, Blackjack, Poker and Keno were the games of chance offered to his clientele. These establishments added to his "capital" if not his fame. This was considered a legitimate business and his reputation in San Diego was good. As a sideline, he acted as a referee for boxing matches.

At night, south of H was a dangerous place to be. It was rife with gangs of hoodlums and juvenile delinquents. Murder was a common occurrence. The City Trustees elected in a "cleanup" campaign in 1887 tried to enforce an 11:00 p.m. curfew, but with little permanent effect. Firearms were considered a necessity for self protection. With so many guns around there were many accidental shootings, especially of children playing with "toy" pistols. Stray dogs and seagulls made convenient targets, and often a passerby got in the way and was struck. It got so bad that finally the city passed some ordinances prohibiting shooting within the city limits or on the bay.

In 1888 Milton Santee, an employee of the California Southern Railroad, for whom the town of Santee was named, was robbed of $10,000 on the train to Los Angeles. This again brought loud protests on the part of the local residents who

Fig. 64 Bum and Friends

Fig. 65 Wyatt Earp

fenders were merely admonished to behave themselves and released to return to their same activities. Finally, in 1888 a new jail was completed and the first occupants, mostly regular boarders, were loud in its praises, in comparison with what had previously been afforded.

A well known alcoholic of the eighties was the town dog, "Bum," who started out as a handsome St. Bernard, born in San Francisco in 1886. He came to San Diego as a stowaway on a steamer and was promptly adopted by Ah Wo Sue. He was a friendly creature and endeared himself to others readily. He was allowed to ride the fire engines to neighborhood fires. The butchers and restaurants always had a handout ready for him. He also found welcome in saloons where patrons were wont to satisfy his thirst. In 1887 he was run over by a Santa Fe train and lost his right front forepaw and part of his tail. Perhaps this depressed him, or gave him so much pain he took to seeking solace more and more from his friends in the saloons. By the time he was four years old he was a confirmed alcoholic. Finally, the Board of Supervisors, in a magnanimous gesture, ordered him to the County Hospital to recover, but he died there instead. San Diego never again had a "town dog."

Many famous persons came to San Diego during the boom days to visit, some even to live here for awhile. But no story of this period would be complete without mention of the celebrated and mysterious Benjamin Henry Jesse Francis Shepard. An ascetic appearing musician with a handlebar mustache, Shepard came to San Diego in 1887 at the age of thirty-eight, a handsome bachelor, and set the town agog. He brought a "culture" the town had not yet experienced. He was a concert pianist, a native of England, and had played before most of the crowned heads of Europe and Russia. He created a furor with his musical seances, and was also a spiritualist. Spiritualism was taking the country by storm at this time. Many San Diegans, including Mrs. Sarah Horton, became interested in the new phenomenon.

Shepard, while in Europe, had become known as a writer, and was a protege of Maurice Maeterlink. When entertaining royalty, he received gifts of art objects and jewelry. In particular, a ring, set with diamonds, was specially made for him by the Court Jeweler in Vienna. His portrait, painted in St. Petersburg, portrayed him with decidedly spiritual features.

Soon after arriving in San Diego he set about building a beautiful home, "Villa Montezuma," at Twentieth and K Streets, which was completed in

deplored the lawlessness, wide open gambling, drinking and prostitution. Unfortunately, they could not seem to get through to public officials, who were lax, and some of whom no doubt were lining their own pockets. The Police Court was always jammed with a backlog of cases. By the time a case could be called the witnesses would have left town. The police were discouraged and said there was no use arresting anybody. The police judge, a Justice of the Peace, was accused of handling civil cases first, for more remunerative fees. The District Attorney, James A. Copeland (1881-91) was considered too lenient. The Union on February 14, 1888, ran this "Valentine":

Sing a song of Copeland, cooler full of thugs;
4 and 20 burglars with their ugly mugs;
Never brought to trial—always ends in fudge,
Isn't this a pretty dish to set before a Judge.

The city's jail was so inadequate that petty of-

the fall of 1887. He claimed it was being built under the direction of the "spirits." It was a veritable palace, built at a cost of $29,000. World travelers who visited in the home marvelled at its interior, saying it surpassed in beauty anything they had seen in the United States or Europe. It was all of hardwood, even the shingles were of black walnut. Rooms contained ebony panels inlaid with bas-relief figures of ivory and mother-of-pearl. The many stained glass windows were of the finest workmanship, exquisite and unique, representing the Four Seasons, and others portraying famous musicians. The furnishings were elaborate and ornate, much of it imported. There were heavy Persian rugs everywhere, and a fine organ as well as a grand piano. The first concert in his home was held on September 22, 1887. It was a big event when a San Diegan could manage an invitation to one of the many musicales and seances held in this home.

Shepard was also a singer, with an unheard of range of voice, four octaves, low C to high C. A reporter wrote of him "His soprano was pure and wonderful; his voice soaring among the higher notes. There is this peculiarity about Jesse Shepard's singing—it thrills as with a voice out of this earth. It is simply indescribable!"

On Christmas, 1887, Shepard played and sang at St. Joseph's Cathedral and it was said he moved the congregation to tears. Another reporter described his singing, "His voice, like a clear, strong soprano, went up without a tremor to high C and held it with a long continued crescendo effect, and his basso was equally as round, full and massive." His hands were unusually large, capable of a great reach on the keyboard.

Although surrounded by apparent wealth and opulence, there was a mystery as to where the money, which flowed to him, was coming from. For his concerts and seances, some of them private, he made a small charge. He wrote occasionally for his friend, Harr Wagner, editor of the monthly magazine *Golden Era*, but other than this, his source of income remained unknown. He credited it to the "spirits," Some who later admitted having contributed, denied it was the spirits, but rather his hypnotism. At his seances he said that the "spirits" spoke to him through sounds coming from the walls. (Later it was claimed there

Fig. 67   Lawrence Tonner served as secretary to Jesse Shepard

were pipes in the walls, which he could unobservedly control, and which caused the eerie sounds.)

A typical seance was described by Vine Bowers Hill, Horton's niece. She said Shepard would play the piano or organ during the seance. At the same time there would be the sounds of tambourines, trumpets, drums, all over the room and from the ceilings. It seemed that voices were coming out of the trumpets (he was a ventriloquist, too). An item of furnishing that impressed her, a young girl, was a large white polar bear rug.

The collapse of the boom had its effect on him. Money was not as easy to come by. His farewell concert in San Diego was in early 1889 at the Unitarian Church in association with Loleta Levet, later Mrs. Thomas E. Rowan.

Father Ubach was instrumental in persuading

Opposite:
Fig. 66   Jesse Francis Shepard

85

Shepard to give up spiritualism, and in 1889 he joined the Catholic Church and moved to Los Angeles. It is said that he confessed that his spiritualistic claims had all been a fake. His last years were spent in poverty, and after his death his most valuable asset was a gold watch inscribed to him from Prince Albert Edward, Prince of Wales (Edward VII).

Still living in San Diego was Mrs. Fidelia Shepherd, Alonzo Horton's cousin, and widow of his confidential assistant, Jesse Shepherd. Mrs. Shepherd, like Mrs. Horton, was interested in spiritualism when it was all the rage. Seances were held in her home and in the Horton mansion. Horton was amused by these antics and took little stock in them, but like a good husband, tolerated them. He did concede to having a crystal ball on his desk, in which he would ask his small nieces

and nephews to look and see what they could see. Possibly as a result of the seances held in the Horton home on First Street, it was later said the house had "spooks" in it.

Mrs. Jesse Shepherd was frequently thought to be the wife or widow of the spiritualist because of the same names, although different spelling. Mrs. Fidelia Shepherd lived in San Diego until her death in 1921. She and her husband are buried in a plot next to the Hortons.

During the boom years, Horton saw his properties increase in value, along with everyone else's, although by now he owned only a fraction of the

Fig. 68 Villa Montezuma

Fig. 69 Grand Union Depot, built in 1886

land he once controlled. By 1888 it was estimated he had given away property then worth over a million dollars, and had spent more than $700,000 of his own money in improvements. One by one, his land was dwindling. He moved his office out of the Horton Bank Block, at Third and D, the control and ownership of which had slipped from his grasp, and opened an office in the new Sun Building on the plaza. The last of his speculative building was a group of cottages and stores on India Street, north of Ash. It was believed this would become the main street leading to Old Town.

But the boom years were happy ones for him and his family, which had increased by marriages and births. Two marriages had taken place in the big front room of his mansion on First Street. The first was that of Mrs. Horton's niece, Amy Brown, who married Dr. Gordon Burleigh of the United States Navy. The second was the very fashionable wedding of his niece, May Horton, to a young attorney, Harry L. Titus, on May 3, 1887. Mr. Titus was for a time City Attorney, and then for years was Chief Counsel to the Spreckels Company. A wedding present from Horton to May Horton Titus was a frame house on Cedar Street, just east of Sixth. He was always very generous to his nieces and nephews. May Horton Titus had come to live with her uncle Alonzo in 1877 at the age of sixteen, and lived with the Hortons until her marriage. She was treated in all respects as a daughter. Horton's brother-in-law, W.W. Bowers, now was State Senator, an office he held from 1887 to 1889.

Although Horton's wealth and influence had diminished, he was still the respected and honored "Father" of San Diego, living in a beautiful mansion on top of the hill. Visiting dignitaries made it a point to travel up First Street to pay their respects to Mr. Horton.

An unfortunate event, for Horton, occurred in 1887. In that year Mrs. Richard S. Proctor, the widow of the famous English astronomer, arrived in San Diego and said she wanted to erect an observatory in this area in her husband's memory. A Mr. Isham, owner of Mt. Miguel, offered the crest of that hill as a possible site. On July 4, a party of twelve men and eight women, Horton included, ascended Mt. Miguel on burros. Their intention was to stay the night, so tents and other gear were taken along. They thought that from the top of this mountain they could watch the fireworks from the city. On the way up, Horton's saddle slipped and he fell into a patch of poison oak. No bones were broken but he was badly shaken up and soon broke out in a painful rash. From that time on he suffered from skin trouble, or an eczema, which gave his complexion a bright pink color.

The group continued to the top of the hill, but that night it was "fogged in" and not a thing could be seen below. Mrs. Proctor wisely decided that it was not a suitable place for her observatory. A flagpole was left at the top of the mountain to mark the visit, and the spot on the trail where Horton fell became known as "Horton's Slide."

Chapter Eleven

The New Subdivisions, 1887–88

The Boom of the Eighties was first and foremost a real estate boom. The growth in business and increase in population was solely a reflection of the hordes who were arriving daily to get in on the land boom. Real estate was still by far the principal business in San Diego. The occupational census of 1888 lists 238 real estate agents in San Diego.

Old residents, like Horton, who had been land poor only a few years before, now began cashing in on the boom, only to turn around and reinvest in other land at inflated prices, sure that their new investments would double or triple in a short time. And often they did. Others who held on a little too long, lost heavily when the boom collapsed.

Along with the big Eastern investors, and the little Midwestern farmer or businessman who came with his life savings hoping to make San Diego his home, were the usual boomers, con men and quick-buck operators. These individuals were often employed by syndicates who bought large tracts of land on speculation and then sent in the fast-talk men to dispose of it, usually to the small investors and home buyers. The ancient motto "Caveat Emptor" (let the buyer beware) was scrupulously followed by the sellers, but all too fre-

Fig. 70 Real estate promotion,
Morena Boulevard, 1888

quently forgotten by the buyers until it was too late.

It was in a circus atmosphere of fun and simulated enthusiasm with which lots in new subdivisions were sold. Brass bands, fireworks, food and drinks, and often a balloon ascension, were a part of the sales pitch. Balloon ascensions were especially popular at Coronado and Pacific Beach, where the air conditions were most favorable. Frequently trapeze and acrobatic stunts were performed from the balloon, to the awe and admiration of the crowds below. Special rigs and coaches were provided to bring people to the sales. There were often auction sales because of the added excitement in bidding. Sometimes bidders did not bother to look at the land on which they were bidding, only at a map. Some lots turned out to be on the side of a hill that not even a goat could climb.

Railroads and streetcar lines were built, to bring

Fig. 71 An advertisement for the new subdivision of University Heights appears along Broadway about 1887

people to where the action was. Along the route of the California Southern the towns of Del Mar, Encinitas, Olivenhain, Carlsbad, Oceanside, Escondido and Fallbrook sprang up. The National City and Otay Railroad ran its first train on January 1, 1887. Its line, when completed, would link San Diego to National City, Otay, Chula Vista and Tijuana, and was built especially to take prospective buyers from San Diego to these new communities. This railroad ran until it was washed out in the 1916 flood.

In 1888 the Cuyamaca & Eastern Railroad was

incorporated to construct a line from San Diego and National City to La Mesa, "the Pasadena of San Diego," and to El Cajon and Lakeside and hopefully on to Needles to connect with the Southern Pacific. It did get as far as Lakeside in 1889. The twenty-six miles of this line became the most traveled railroad in San Diego county. Governor Waterman became its sole owner in 1890.

The Lakeside Inn, a three story hotel with eighty rooms on Lake Lindo, opened in 1887. Until the railroad arrived in 1889, there was a daily stage to San Diego taking four hours. After the railroad came, business boomed and in 1906 an automobile race track was built. It was there that Barney Oldfield is supposed to have set his first world's speed record. The old Victorian style hotel was torn down in 1920.

The beach areas, long popular as picnic spots, were prime targets for the land developers and speculators, with Coronado setting an example. Ocean Beach, first known as Mussel Beach, was where the Old Towners went to gather mussels and bathe. This beach was later discovered by New Towners, in spite of the long journey of several hours by wagon. Mussel bakes became popular for Sunday School picnics. While the parents were gathering mussels, the children would be entertained by bobbing for apples placed in pot holes in the rocks. The mussel beds extended from Narragansett to Santa Cruz. An abalone cave was at the foot of Del Mar.

In 1886 there arrived in San Diego, along with other real estate promoters, another colorful personality, William (Billy) Carlson, who opened a real estate and insurance office on Fifth, between F and G. In April of 1887 he and a partner, Frank J. Higgins, acquired a tract of land bounded by Froude, Brighton, Point Loma Boulevard and the ocean, and set out a new subdivision called Ocean Beach. This tract had been offered for sale in 1885 for $500, but there were no takers. It wasn't worth it.

Carlson and Higgins then began an extensive advertising campaign. Among the glowing promises were that "one of the finest hotels in the state" would be built at Ocean Beach and the electric street railroad would be extended to the hotel. To make the story even better, a railroad would be built from Ocean Beach to connect with the Southern Pacific so that easterners could go directly to Ocean Beach, where Ponce de Leon, if only he had come to California instead of Florida, would have found his Fountain of Youth. Advertisements claimed "Ocean Beach is destined to be the greatest seaside resort in Southern California."

This first big sale of lots was on Sunday, April 24, 1887. The promoters provided a mussel roast, ice cream and even bathing suits for those who came unprepared for a dip. The City Guard Band, under the direction of Jack Dodge, was on hand for a concert to keep the spirits up. Transportation was provided from San Diego. One thousand people attended and 2500 lots were sold, many at $60 each, $20 down and the balance payable in one year.

To continue sales at Ocean Beach, the promoters provided a four-horse stage which left from their office each day at 8:00 a.m. and 1:00 p.m. for a nominal fifty cent fare. By October, the average price of lots had gone up to $300. On August 21, 1887, another Grand Barbecue (mussel roast and clam bake) was provided by the promoters. This time four thousand attended.

The promised hotel opened early in 1888. It was located at the foot of Niagara, and known as the Cliff House. It was a three-story, frame building with an octagonal tower, gabled roof, arched balustrade and large balcony. Carlson claimed it cost $85,000. Whatever the cost, it fulfilled the promises of the promoter to the satisfaction of all viewers and became a popular tourist hotel for summer visitors. In April, 1888, a gala Founders' Day celebration was held, honoring not only Carlson and Higgins, founders of Ocean Beach, but also Alonzo E. Horton, founder of New San Diego, who was one of the speakers.

In 1889 there was a minor "gold rush" to Ocean Beach, after Carlson claimed he turned up some gold nuggets on the beach. Several visitors also reported finding some. This excitement did not last long. A good guess is that the nuggets, if real, were "planted."

Transportation to Ocean Beach was difficult and holding up sales; so Carlson promoted a railroad from Old Town to Roseville and over the hill to Ocean Beach. Its first run was on April 17, 1888, with a borrowed locomotive. It promptly got mired in mud. Carlson, along with other dignitaries in frock coats and top hats, was obliged to climb out and dig in order to get the train back on the tracks. After a few runs, the line threw in the sponge. In 1890, the Pacific Coast Steamship Company attached the rails on a rental claim for the "borrowed" steam engine. Carlson and Higgins then built a wharf at the foot of G Street and established a ferry

Fig. 72 Promotional piece for the new townsite of Lakeside

This Hotel is under contract to be finished January next.

Cost of Hotel Plant, $50,000!

Lands of El Cajon Valley Company,

Including the noted "Benedict tract" of 6,000 acres, are now being surveyed and placed on the market in subdivisions of ten acres and upwards. It stands unequaled in soil, climate and scenery. All fruits of Southern California grow here to perfection, WITHOUT IRRIGATION, and this land is specially suited for the raisin grape and olive. A railroad is now under construction to

LAKESIDE.

The Company has surveyed and laid off on this tract, adjacent to the lake, a townsite called Lakeside, overlooking lake, river, valley and hills. Water Works. Mountain Spring Water is being piped over the tract. The new mesa road will make a short, pleasant drive to El Cajon valley and Lakeside. The locality is notably healthful and wonderfully picturesque. All deeds prohibit the sale of liquors. Pamphlets with maps and plats of subdivisions at office and at Lakeside Hotel. Hotel now open. Daily stages and telephone.

E. W. Morse, President; G. H. Mansfield, Vice-President; O. S. Hubbell, Second Vice-President; Consolidated National Bank, Treasurer; I. M. Merrill, Secretary. We refer to First National Bank and to the Consolidated National Bank.

PIERCE-MORSE BLOCK, SAN DIEGO, CAL.

Fig. 73 The Cliff House, Ocean
Beach, 1888

service between San Diego and Roseville. At Roseville there was a connecting stage to Ocean Beach.

With all these promotion activities, Carlson succeeded also in promoting himself for Mayor of San Diego. He was elected and served from 1893 to 1896. Because of his youth (he was only twenty-one when he arrived in San Diego), he was called the "Boy Mayor."

In the nineties, when almost all the Boom Town hotels burned down, the Cliff House at Ocean Beach was no exception. It burned in 1894 with a heavy loss, but was rebuilt with insurance money and continued for a number of years as a place for summer tourists. Also lost in the fire were the records of all land sales in the subdivision. However, at the time of the fire, Carlson and Higgins were no longer the owners.

Carlson and Higgins were also promoters of Monument City, advertised as "the southwest corner of the United States." Their advertisements pictured a huge hotel "guaranteed to be finished before September 26, 1888." Lots were sold for $100 to $500, on the promise of the hotel and a direct train line from San Diego. This turned out to be just another paper town. The monument at the southwest corner of the United States stands today as bleak and lonely as it did then.

Great things were also promised by the promoters of Pacific Beach, another beach subdivision laid out in 1887. Pacific Beach was to be an educational center, the home of the San Diego College of Letters. Up to that time, San Diego offered no higher education for the children of its residents. The few who could afford it were obliged to go north or east to college.

Among the Pacific Beach promoters was Harr Wagner, editor and publisher of the *Golden Era*, a monthly magazine established in San Francisco in 1852. In 1887 Wagner opened an office at Seventh and H and started publication of the magazine in San Diego. At the same time he began a campaign for "culture" in San Diego, something obviously lacking in the little community. The *Golden Era* was known as *the* literary journal of the Southwest. It contained articles on travel, general literature and fiction. It was the oldest illustrated magazine on the Pacific Coast.

In January, 1888, the cornerstone was laid for the San Diego College of Letters, located at Lamont and Garnet Streets. Joaquin Miller, "The Poet of the Sierras," was the speaker. The college would offer "classical, scientific and literary courses." Its grounds were to cover seventeen acres. The college opened with great fanfare in the fall, with one building completed. The faculty of fourteen was headed by Harr Wagner. The college, however, was of short duration. With the collapse of the boom, it folded. The building then became a hotel—The Balboa—and in more recent years was the site of a military academy. It is now a shopping center. Harr Wagner continued to publish the *Golden Era* in San Diego until 1895. From 1889 until 1894 he served as County Superintendent of Schools. In 1895 he moved back to San Francisco and the name of the *Golden Era* was changed to the *Western Journal of Education.*

San Diego's race track, popular in the eighties, was at the foot of Rose Canyon on False Bay, now approximately between Garnet and Grand, at Mission Bay Drive. One of the most noteworthy events at the race track occurred in the same month the College of Letters opened. It was a broadsword contest on horseback, billed as "The Great Jaguarine-Weidermann Fight." The contest was sponsored by Concordia Turnverein, a German sports club organized in 1886. It was so well publicized that a large crowd turned out to witness the unusual event, on Sunday, October 28. Weidermann was the physical instructor for the Turnverein and an instructor in fencing and boxing. His opponent was a famous, or notorious, female known as The Great Jaguarine. She was an American, but had been living in Ensenada, and recently had won a broadsword contest with the United States Navy champion. She arrived in San Diego on horseback in full regalia. She was a large, husky, good looking woman, with dark hair and eyes and a fair complexion.

Weidermann was easily the favorite of the crowd, who could not believe a mere woman could topple this giant of a man. When they appeared in the ring, each on a big horse, masked, helmeted, with swords flashing, and their breastplates shining in the sun, it was a sight to see, a thrilling spectacle. After eleven "attacks" of three minutes each, it was The Great Jaguarine who was declared the winner.

It is to Concordia Turnverein, and to one of its later instructors, Theodore Treutlein, that the San Diego City Schools owe their first physical culture instruction. Treutlein was for years in charge of the Physical Education program in the city schools, using the German system of dumbbell exercise, club swinging and calisthenics.

In 1887 the San Diego & Old Town Electric Railway built a railroad to go from San Diego, starting at D and Arctic (Kettner), going out Arctic to Old Town. It was to use overhead power lines, one of the first in the United States. Its first run was in October, 1887, using a coal burner "dummy" engine. The overhead wires were first used in November. These were soon removed for use on the new Fourth Street line in San Diego, and the Old Town railroad went back to steam engines. In 1888, with the boom in Pacific Beach, this line became the San Diego & Pacific Beach Railway and was extended around False Bay to the racetrack, the College of Letters and out Grand Avenue to the ocean where an elaborate dance pavilion was constructed, on the present Crystal Pier site. The round trip fare was fifteen cents to Old Town and twenty-five cents to Pacific Beach. This line was plagued by floods. In December, 1889, a flood wiped out the race track and much of the railroad tracks, and in March, 1893, another flood hit the railroad and destroyed the San Diego river bridge.

Pacific Beach grew slowly, along the route of the railway. In the nineties a lemon boom started in Pacific Beach. For a time it had a large lemon packing house, which shipped lemons in carload lots. It also boasted an asbestos factory, the asbestos coming from nearby Elsinore.

Mission Bay was known as False Bay until Harr Wagner and his *Golden Era* magazine conducted a contest to rename it. It was Wagner who pointed out that False Bay, in its formation, was almost an exact facsimile, in miniature, of San Diego Bay.

The contest was won by Rose Hartwick Thorpe, and the first use of the name Mission Bay was in

Fig. 74 Ocean Beach visitors

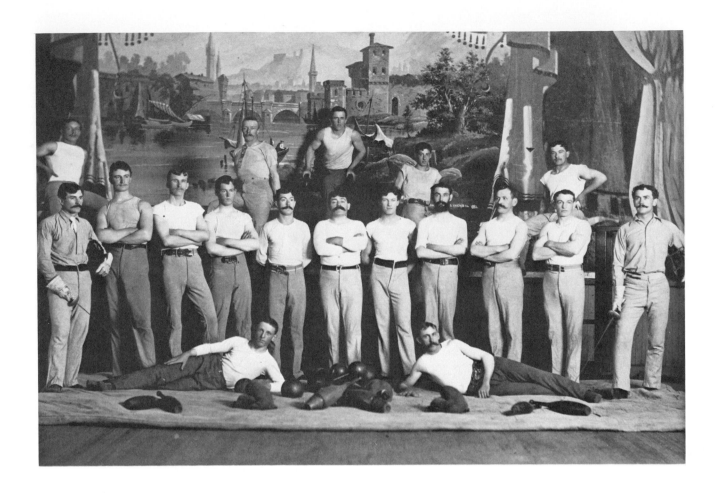

Fig. 75 Concordia Turnverein,
German sports club
organized in 1886

her poem, published in the August, 1888, issue of
Golden Era:

Beyond the bay the city lies
White-walled beneath the azure skies,
So far remote, no sounds of it
Across the peaceful waters flit—
Fair Mission Bay
Now blue, now gray,
Now flushed by sunset's afterglow.

La Jolla was the third beach subdivision to go on
the market in 1887. La Jolla, with its fascinating
caves, rock formations, and its famous Cathedral
Rock, since disintegrated, was a popular picnic
spot in spite of the long distance from San Diego.

In 1886 Frank T. Botsford bought La Jolla. He and
a partner, George W. Heald, subdivided it under
the name of The Pacific Coast Land Bureau. The
first auction of lots was on April 30, 1887, with all
the usual fanfare and extravagant promises, one of
which was that good water had already been piped
in from wells in Rose Canyon. This, of course, was
only a "pipe" dream. The usual promises of a hotel
and railroad were also made.

The shores of La Jolla were compared with the
coastline of the Mediterranean. In the first few
days, $56,000 worth of lots were sold. The land
above the cliffs was completely barren. Botsford
and Heald planted over one thousand trees,
eucalyptus, cedar and palm. Many died from lack
of water, but of those that managed to survive,
some still remain to add to the beauty of La Jolla.
Both Botsford and Heald built homes for
themselves in La Jolla, and lived there for a while,
something not usually done by promoters.

Five little cottages were built on Prospect Street,

94

one of which became known as La Jolla Park Cottage Hotel, until the promised hotel could be built. Work was started on the La Jolla Park Hotel on Girard Avenue. It was an eighty room, three-story edifice, with a big veranda. The cost of the hotel was said to be $18,000. Unfortunately, the boom burst about the time it was completed, payments could not be made and litigation kept the hotel from opening. It stood in all its forlorn splendor until 1892 when a former operator of the Royal Hawaiian Hotel in Honolulu took it over. It was opened with a Grand Ball and entertainment on January 1, 1893.

Transportation to La Jolla was a problem until the San Diego, Old Town & Pacific Beach Railway extended its line to La Jolla in 1894. On May 15 its completion was celebrated with a picnic. Excursion trains left San Diego every hour that day. The City Guard Band was again on hand for a concert. The run from San Diego to La Jolla took exactly one hour, including stops at Old Town and Pacific Beach, cutting in half the horse and buggy time. This railway was in operation until 1917.

The hotel benefited from this new transportation. For a few years it was a popular holiday hotel, with the usual dances and special events, but the operators never could make it profitable and it was forced to close in February, 1896.

The failure of these hotels, in Ocean Beach and La Jolla, was due in part to the nationwide depression of the early nineties and also to Babcock and Story's Hotel del Coronado, which with all its splendor was something these smaller hotels could not have competed with even in better times. On June 14, 1896, the La Jolla Park Hotel burned to the ground. This seemed to happen to all the "boom" hotels, one by one. By coincidence, they were all heavily insured.

Other subdivisions, north and east of the city, were also being set out during these boom years. University Heights was opened in 1887 by College Hill Land Association. These promoters, instead of promising a grand hotel, said they would build the San Diego College of Arts. The fact that Pacific Beach was to have a College of Letters did not seem to deter them. What with the increase in population expected, along with continued prosperity, there was room for more than one college.

The College Hill Land Association agreed to sell lots for one-fourth down and the balance in two years, at ten percent interest, providing the purchaser agreed to build a house costing not less than $1000, within ninety days. A number of houses were built in this tract, located north of

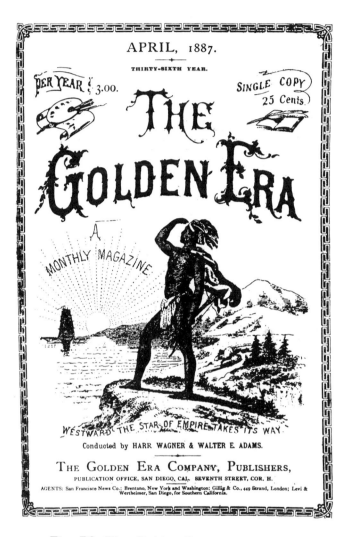

Fig. 76 The *Golden Era* magazine was published in San Diego from 1887 to 1895

University Avenue and west of Park Boulevard, extending to the rim of Mission Valley. Driving through these streets today, one can identify some of those homes built during the boom of the eighties. It would be ten years before a college actually was built in that area.

This same company also laid out Grantville, named for the general and later president. The promotion idea here was that a G.A.R. Soldiers' Home would be built which would be able to boast "the very finest climate," particularly suited to the senior citizen, then frankly referred to as "old people." Lots were advertised for $100, with $25 down. Not many were sold, and the proposed soldiers' home was soon forgotten.

University Heights was helped by a streetcar service. The Electric Rapid Transit Street Car Company began service in 1887 from the foot of Fifth to K, then to Fourth, north to Palm, east to Fifth and north to Upas. In 1888 it was extended out along a county road to University Heights.

East San Diego, or City Heights, was another boom-time subdivision given impetus by a street

Fig. 77 The La Jolla Park Hotel on Girard Avenue had three stories and eighty rooms

Fig. 78 Driving the last spike in the La Jolla and Pacific Beach Railroad

railway service. In 1888 the Park Belt Motor Railroad, another Babcock and Story enterprise, started operating from Eighteenth and A, at the foot of Switzer's Canyon (Pershing Drive). It went northeast through the canyons, under what would later be the Thirtieth Street Bridge, to Marlborough, then to University Avenue, back to Fifth and downtown. The "train" consisted of a dummy engine borrowed from the Coronado line, with a horse car hooked on behind. Three trains a day were promised. The promoters of City Heights succeeded in disposing of eight hundred lots at $200 to $400, but by then the boom had become a bust. With a decrease in activity this line was soon dropped and the rails were abandoned. Portions of the track have been found in the canyons in recent years.

During the last months of 1887, total sales of real property in the county sometimes ran more than $200,000 in a day. The population was estimated to be around 40,000. One realty ad read: "We may say that San Diego has a population of 150,000, only they are not all here yet."

Chapter Twelve

In the Wake of the Boom, 1888–89

By January, 1888, the Hotel del Coronado was nearing completion and San Diegans were anxiously awaiting its "Grand Opening." Coronado had become known as "The best advertised property in the United States." Babcock and Story, with their personal influence, were selling Coronado to their wealthy friends in the East, not only as a vacation resort, but as a place in which to retire or invest. For employees of the hotel, they brought from Boston highly specialized and experienced cooks, waiters, doormen, housekeepers and office personnel.

The official opening of the hotel was on February 19. It was the grand social event all San Diegans had been waiting for, attended by social greats from far and near. Special trains came from the East bringing guests to "one of the most fashionable hotels in the world."

The huge dining room, 156 feet long, 62 feet wide, and 33 feet high, was capable of seating one thousand. With its sugar pine panelling, its Crown Jewel lighting, and not a single pillar to obstruct the diner's vision, it was breath-takingly beautiful and an architectural marvel.

The cost of the hotel and its elaborate furnishings was well over one million dollars. It had all the modern conveniences, water, gas for lighting, telephones, and even a telegraph office for the convenience of its important guests. It boasted 73 bathrooms for its 399 bedrooms. Each bedroom contained an open grate, using wood or coal, and a wall safe, for the comfort of the guests and safety of their valuables.

Rates by the day were $3.00 and up. For those who remained a week, the minimum was $2.50 per day, and for a month, $2.00 per day. Among the hotel's first distinguished guests was President Benjamin Harrison.

Credit for the beauty of the building goes to the architects, James W. Reid and Merritt Reid, brothers, of Evansville, Indiana. Instructions to the architects were a minimum, only that the hotel should be built around a large garden court. Redwood lumber was used, shipped from San Francisco. Labor was the major problem. As much skilled and unskilled labor as could be found was employed from San Diego. Then several hundred Chinese were hired from San Francisco. All this unskilled labor had to be given on-the-job training by the few experienced workers available. The tremendous amount of highly decorative woodwork, much of it hand carved, is all the more amazing when one realizes it was done by previously unskilled hands, and the resulting masterpiece of handcraftsmanship is to the credit of these painstaking workers.

Three ferries traveled between San Diego and Coronado, one leaving every twenty minutes from the foot of H to connect on the other side with the train of the Coronado Belt Line, taking the passengers to the hotel. The first ferries were the *Coronado, Benicia,* and *Silver Gate.* The *Silver Gate* proved to be top heavy and unmanageable, and after it tore out pilings on the wharf it became an excursion boat for a time, and then was moored off Coronado and converted into a dance hall. It later sank during a windstorm.

Electricity came to the hotel in 1894 when Thomas A. Edison personally supervised its in-

Opposite:
Fig. 79 Hotel del Coronado under
       construction

Fig. 80 Hotel del Coronado, 1888

stallation. It became the largest structure outside New York City to be lighted by electricity.

Early in 1888 the first rumors began that all was not well, that this prosperity could not last forever and perhaps a crash was in the offing. Speculators and investors became fewer, and soon there was a "save yourself" atmosphere. By April, it was apparent to even the most unbelieving, the boom was over. And this was true throughout Southern California. The Great Land Boom had lasted about eighteen months, from the summer of 1886 to February, 1888. The lovely dream now became a nightmare. People could not leave fast enough. Many lost everything. Others sold just enough to get out of town. Within a few months, the population dropped to 16,000. During that time, two million dollars had been withdrawn from local banks, leaving them in a precarious condition.

Again, as it was with the collapse of the boom of the early seventies, there was a "sieving" of the population. Those who managed to weather the financial storm and liked it here, remained to plod

Fig. 81 Charles Reinhart's sketch of strollers at Coronado Beach accompanied a breathtaking story about San Diego's new hotel in *Harper's Weekly*

along, gradually building and improving their city, confident that with all its attributes, it would one day be a great city. Even if it did not, that was all right. They still liked it as a place to live.

Now, when it appeared that people with money were leaving San Diego as fast as they could, there appeared on the scene as a financial "angel," the one who, after Horton, became the most influential man in San Diego, John D. Spreckels. However, unlike Horton who had only modest means when he founded San Diego, Spreckels had millions at his disposal. He was the son of Claus Spreckels, the "Sugar King" of Hawaii and San Francisco.

In 1887, while on a pleasure cruise down the coast from San Francisco on his luxury yacht, the *Lurline*, the provisions on board ran low and it was decided to land in San Diego, not a planned stop. When San Diego officials learned that the millionaire "Sugar Prince" and his party were about to enter San Diego Bay, a delegation was quickly formed to greet them. Spreckels was prevailed upon to take a tour of San Diego, and there were recounted to him all the grand expectations of the booming community. He was impressed with what he saw, especially with the plans for Coronado and its fabulous hotel. Perhaps he thought of it as a West Coast rival to his beloved Honolulu.

When the town's businessmen began pointing out investment opportunities, he listened. One offer especially appealed to him, and that was a wharf franchise. He decided to build a wharf for coal bunkers, for the use of the Santa Fe which was threatening to terminate its line to San Diego because of a lack of coal. He constructed a wharf at the foot of G, completed in 1889 at a cost of $90,000. The capacity of the coal bunkers was 15,000 gross tons. Tracks were then laid from the wharf to the railroad. The Santa Fe line was saved.

The Spreckels family in San Francisco did not approve of his business venture in San Diego, and could not understand why he wanted to waste his money or time in San Diego. But he and his brother, Adolph, who had formed a partnership as the Spreckels Brothers Commercial Company, went ahead with the venture. Although Adolph Spreckels never took the same interest in San Diego as did his brother, he never questioned John D.'s judgment or investment, and during their lives they operated on a strictly fifty-fifty basis.

With the collapse of the boom, Babcock and Story found themselves in financial difficulties. When their hotel was threatened with foreclosure, they accepted a loan of $100,000 from Spreckels in order to keep it open. This loan was never repaid. The Spreckels Brothers then bought into the Coronado Beach Company, and purchased the Coronado Belt Line and the Ferry Company. Within a few years, Spreckels would take over most of the Babcock and Story interests. E.S. Babcock remained in San Diego for many years, but, like Horton, would see others acquire great wealth from what he had started, while he himself would die comparatively poor. In 1903 Spreckels assumed complete ownership of the Hotel del Coronado, and all unsold lots in Coronado, as well as the Silver Strand and North Island. Up to that time, North Island was used by the hotel guests as a place to hunt rabbits.

During the boom years many changes occurred in the city government. It had moved from a Sixth Class to a Fourth Class City, and in 1888 a new City Charter was voted to take effect in 1889. Under the new Charter, San Diego would have an elected Mayor, the first since 1852. From 1852 until 1889, the President of the Board of Trustees performed the duties of Mayor. Elected Mayor was Douglas Gunn, a former editor of the *San Diego Union*, and brother-in-law of George W. Marston and Charles S. Hamilton.

Instead of the old five-man Board of Trustees, the city would now be run by eighteen men and the Mayor. There were nine Aldermen, elected at

Fig. 82 John D. Spreckels

101

Fig. 83 Engine Company Number
One, Fifth between C and D
Streets

large, and nine Delegates, elected by Ward. City elections were on a partisan basis.

The Charter set up new city offices and departments, and therefore larger quarters were needed to house this expanding city government. The Horton Bank Building at the corner of Third and D now became the City Hall and provided adequate space for offices for the Mayor, City Auditor, Chief of Police, Board of Public Works, City Health Officer, City Engineer, City Clerk, City Attorney, City Tax Collector, as well as chambers for the meetings of the Board of Aldermen and Board of Delegates. There was no question but with all these offices,

San Diego was getting to be a big city.

San Diego now had a Police Department, organized May 16, 1889. Before this, Constables had been the law enforcement officers. Joseph Coyne became the first Chief of Police, with thirty men on his staff. It would be 1909 before a Traffic Division would be set up. That was one problem early police officers did not have to cope with. But they had plenty of others, particularly maintaining law and order in the Stingaree District. One of the first accomplishments of the new Mayor and Chief of Police was to close down some of the more notorious dance halls and gambling establishments.

Also in 1889, San Diego acquired its first paid Fire Department, when a Board of Fire Commissioners was appointed. There were now three engine companies, and sixty-five hydrants, located strategically throughout the central area. Equipment consisted of one La France Steam Fire Engine, two four-wheel hose carts, one two-wheel hose cart, one hook and ladder truck and 1750 feet of hose.

The fire alarm consisted of one bell located on a tower over San Diego Engine Company #1, on the east side of Fifth between C and D. The city was divided into six fire alarm districts. Directions were: "Ring bell rapidly to give general alarm. Then toll the bell the same number of times as the number of the district in which the fire is located."

Just how one was expected to notify the fire department of a fire, in the absence of a telephone, was not explained. Perhaps a runner was used. And as for locating the fire, we must presume the firemen on occasion had to use their eyes and noses. Volunteers were still called upon in emergencies. In 1909 motorization came to the Fire Department, the same year the Police Department established its traffic division.

By 1889 all the downtown streets had been paved, from the waterfront east to Twelfth and north to Date. Cement sidewalks also were laid, but instead of a pleased citizenry, the city fathers were besieged with complaints—the white sidewalks caused a ter-

Fig. 84 Courthouse with 1888 additions

rific glare. As a result, a darkening substance was added to later sidewalks. In 1894, grading was extended out D to Twenty-Fifth and north on Sixth from Date to Upas.

Also, thanks to the boom, San Diego could afford its first sewer system. In 1886, $400,000 in bonds were voted to construct sewers. Before this, cesspools were in use. Sanitary conditions were appalling, even for those days. Diptheria was common and there were several smallpox epidemics. The only precautionary measure taken by the city to protect citizens against serious epidemics was to provide a place of isolation for those infected, euphemistically called the Pest House. In the eighties there was a smallpox scare and a Pest House was built at the north end of Switzer Canyon. It was equipped with sixteen beds and the necessary furnishings. When not in use, the building was left unattended. It was thought to be too far out of town to be molested. A few years later, when someone thought to take a look at it, the furnishings were gone and there was evidence that a beekeeper had been using it.

In 1885 the Board of Trustees had established a Department of Sanitation, Sewer and Scavenger. Garbage was collected, loaded on barges and dumped at sea. By 1889, forty-seven miles of

Fig. 85 B Street School, Sixth and
B Streets, built in 1888

Fig. 86 Russ School

sewer had been laid, from the waterfront to
Twenty-Fourth Street. This amounted to 211,560
feet of pipe. Such a good job was done that this
sewer system lasted for many years.

The County offices, too, had suffered growing
pains, and it was necessary to enlarge the courthouse. More than $100,000 was spent in remodel-
ing and enlarging the courthouse and jail. The
courthouse now was topped with a gilded statue of
Justice, complete with blindfold and scales. Also,
it was adorned by four life-sized statues of
Washington, Lincoln, Grant and Garfield. The

statues were said to be not very good likenesses
and were derisively called "mud statues." They
were later removed. It would be interesting to
know if any of these statues still exist, hidden away
in some garage or junk shop.

The boom, short as it was, left many lasting
benefits to the city. It was estimated ten million
dollars had been expended in San Diego in two
years. Fifteen large business buildings had been
constructed, as well as new homes, churches and
schools. In Florence Heights alone, more than one
hundred homes had been built, pushing the
residential area north to the edge of Mission
Valley, so that in 1889 Mission Hills Addition was
opened up as a fashionable new residential district.

The juvenile population had boomed along with

Fig. 87 Mrs. Sarah Horton in later years

everything else. In 1886 the total public school enrollment was 716, with eleven teachers, an average of sixty-five pupils per teacher. However, the school year was only eight months.

In 1888 three beautiful new grammar school buildings were built, almost identical in appearance. A larger Sherman School was built at Seventeenth and H, also on land donated by Matthew Sherman. A new school, the Middletown, was erected at 1825 State Street, and the Little Pink Schoolhouse at Sixth and B was moved down to Eleventh and J where it became a Kindergarten. The new school building at Sixth and B became officially the B Street School. In 1890 another school was built in Logan Heights, to become known as the East School.

In 1882 Joseph Russ, owner of the Russ Lumber Company, offered to donate lumber for a new school, to be built on park land near Thirteenth and A. The school, built at a cost of $18,428.73, inclusive of the donated lumber, opened August 14, 1882, with 276 pupils, and was named Russ School. It contained all grades at first, but in January, 1888, it became a high school and later was renamed San Diego High School. The first principal was J.A. Rice. One of the first teachers was Miss Kate O. Sessions, an attractive young woman and recent graduate of the University of California at Berkeley. However, she soon discovered teaching was not for her. For one thing, she was unable to maintain discipline, particularly among the big boys who liked to tease and annoy her. After some boys, as a prank, locked her up with some other women teachers who were attending a meeting, she decided she had had enough of teaching and would devote her time to her real interest, horticulture. In 1887 when Coronado was being developed, she moved there and opened her first nursery, the Coronado Nursery. Many of the first plantings around the Hotel del Coronado were from her nursery. For a number of years she maintained a florist stand in the courtyard of the hotel, selling cut flowers. She never had any trouble disciplining her plants and flowers, who became her "children." The schools' loss was the city's gain, for the name Kate O. Sessions would become one of the "greats" in the world of horticulture.

San Diego's "seemingly inexhaustible" supply of water in the seventies was not enough to supply the mushrooming population of the eighties. In 1886, work was commenced on Sweetwater Dam and reservoir, completed in 1888. In the same year, the Otay Water Company was formed, to build Morena and Otay Dams. This company later

Fig. 88 Riding the flume, February
22, 1889

became the Southern California Mountain Water Company. It was the Babcock interests that furnished the money for these South Bay Water developments. When completed they would serve National City, Chula Vista and Coronado. In 1889 Babcock took over the old San Diego Water Company. These water companies soon passed into the hands of the Spreckels Company, and in 1896 the Southern California Mountain Water Company was acquired by the city, but not without much controversy.

Also in 1886, the San Diego Flume Company was organized, for the purpose of bringing water from Lake Cuyamaca to the city. A reservoir was built at Cuyamaca, and thirty-five miles of flume built, ending west of El Cajon. From there water was brought through pipes to La Mesa, Lemon Grove, Spring Valley and San Diego. The wooden flume was six feet wide and four feet high. It required 315 trestles to carry the flume through

valleys and canyons. Gravity was the only propellant. It was promised the water would be clear and fresh, not brackish, as had been the well water then in use.

A great celebration was planned on Washington's Birthday 1889, the date on which the first Cuyamaca water was to arrive in San Diego. Governor Robert W. Waterman was on hand, as well as Mayor Gunn and other dignitaries, who coasted down the flume in glass bottomed boats, at a speed much faster than had been anticipated. Their hair-raising trip of several miles probably was the first roller coaster ride in San Diego.

In town, thousands were on hand to view the parade, which started at 2:00 p.m. at Sixth and H. In the first carriage were Bryant Howard, the Chairman of the Day, and Alonzo E. Horton, the Vice-Chairman. At Fifth and Ivy a grandstand had been erected, and here a jet spray "visible over the entire city" was to announce the arrival of the water. While the crowd was waiting, those in charge discovered the water was not coming through. Air bubbles had caused the delay and the water was still three miles away. Rather than disappoint the waiting citizenry, it was decided to turn on the old water supply. As the spray came on everyone rejoiced, and those who sampled it were enthusiastic in their praise, it tasted much better than the old well water they were used to! One orator could not contain his rapture: "It means our San Diego, our loved San Diego, the Pearl of the Southern Sea, shall be seen in emerald, and become the most beautiful city in all the earth!" The San Diego Flume Company was taken over in 1910 by Ed Fletcher and James A. Murray, and became the Cuyamaca Water Company.

Governor Waterman, the distinguished, bearded gentleman in the front seat of the "roller coaster" on that February 22, 1889, had become closely identified with San Diego County. In 1886 he purchased the Stonewall Mine, near Julian, for $45,000. It was idle at the time and thought to be exhausted. It was reactivated and yielded over $900,000 in ore by the time of his death. He also purchased the entire Cuyamaca Grant on which it was located. His cattle ranch later became Cuyamaca State Park. In 1887, while Lieutenant Governor, he succeeded to the office of Governor upon the death of Governor Washington Bartlett, and served until January 8, 1891. He made his home in San Diego in a beautiful house at First and Kalmia, which still stands in a state of perfect preservation. Waterman died of pneumonia in his San Diego home on April 12, 1891, and is buried in Mount Hope Cemetery.

The collapse of the boom was disastrous to Horton, and for a man less optimistic in nature, could have resulted in a complete breakdown in spirit and in health. Horton was now seventy-five years of age, but still mentally keen and remarkably full of energy. Nevertheless, the likelihood of regaining even a small part of the fortune he had made and lost was now remote, although he always remained confident that his fortunes would pick up, just as they always had in the past. During the next few years, some of his remaining properties slipped through his fingers at delinquent tax sales and by foreclosure. He was a drowning man, hanging on desperately, but without ever giving up hope. As if financial troubles were not enough, tragedy also struck. Mrs. Sarah Horton, while visiting her niece, Amy Burleigh, in Washington, D.C., on May 17, 1889, was thrown from a carriage and instantly killed. She was sixty-nine years of age. The *San Diego Union* on May 18, in reporting the accident, said: "This sad news will be received in this community with a genuine expression of regret. Her many lovable qualities had endeared her to a large circle of friends. Sen. Bowers received the news. She left San Diego two weeks previously to visit her niece, Mrs. Dr. Burleigh, in Washington, D.C." Horton was visiting in Elsinore at the time. Her body was returned to San Diego for burial in Mount Hope Cemetery, beside Horton's parents.

The year 1889 came to a close with Horton alone in his big white mansion on First Street, with his city mushrooming around him, but no longer under his direction or control.

Fig. 89   Fourth and Elm, after the Boom, Florence Hotel is on the left

Chapter Thirteen

The Not So Gay Nineties, 1890–99

Soon after becoming a widower, Horton decided to put his big home on the market. It was too big for him, and he had begun to feel the pinch of the depression. He was hurt financially more by the collapse of the boom than he had been by any of his other financial ups and downs. He was now retired, dealing only occasionally in sales of his own property. He looked for another location to build his last home. This time he went out of Horton's Addition, and in August, 1889, purchased the north half of Block 101 of Middletown, between Columbia and State, at Olive. This was way, way out, north of Laurel, on the hill overlooking the bay. The area around was completely unimproved.

Horton was now seventy-six years of age, but still young in heart. After being widowed twice, he took for himself another wife. The lady who would be the last Mrs. Horton was Mrs. Lydia M. Knapp, a widow, with two grown sons. On November 21, 1890, Horton and Mrs. Knapp were married in the home of their good friends, Mr. and Mrs. E.W. Morse, at Ninth and G. Streets.

The *Union*, on November 22, wrote of the wedding:

"The Founder of San Diego Scores Another Stroke of Luck—The founder of San Diego, A.E. Horton, whom every man, woman and child knows as "Father" Horton, took unto himself yesterday for the handsome mansion on the heights, a bride who will adorn it by her natural graces and high cultivation. Mrs. Lydia Maria Knapp is known best here in the Unitarian circle, having resigned the Superintendency of the Sunday School only last week. As art instructor of the Southwest Institute for two years, her skill has spoken for itself. The ceremony was held at the Morse residence. Judge John D. Works, Associate Justice of the State Supreme Court, officiated, and Mr. and Mrs. Morse stood up with them. Roses perfumed the parlor where the party of five sat down to lunch. Then Mr. and Mrs. Horton took the four o'clock train to Los Angeles where they intend to visit Arrowhead and other resorts and will return in ten days. He is thirty years senior of the bride, but is young in heart and certain he will live to see San Diego the metropolis of the coast."

No two women could have been more different in temperament and personality than Sarah Horton and Lydia Knapp. Almost nothing is known about Sarah Horton except that she was a devoted, loyal wife for nearly thirty years, a charming hostess, although always remaining in the background. In contrast, Mrs. Lydia Horton was a woman of dominant character and strong persuasion. She had been obliged to support herself and her two young sons for many years, not an easy task in those times.

Fig. 90 Lydia Maria Knapp Horton

Fig. 91 Horton residence on State Street

Lydia Knapp Horton was born at Newburyport, Massachusetts. In 1866 she married Lieutenant William Knapp of the United States Navy. In 1868 she sailed with her first son to San Francisco via Panama. The Knapps lived at the Presidio where a second son was born. Shortly after that, Lieutenant Knapp was transferred to San Diego, where they lived at Roseville in a house built by Louis Rose for a hotel, but never used as such. The only people living in Roseville were whalers and fishermen. Rose had hoped to establish a city there, and built a hotel on the dirt road which later became Rosecrans Street. In 1870, Lieutenant Knapp built a small frame house for his family, and in 1871 it was towed across the bay and located on Tenth Street in up and coming New Town. It was then that the Knapps and Hortons became friends, and were among the founders of the Unitarian Society.

In the early eighties, Lieutenant Knapp and his family were sent back to San Francisco, where they lived until his death in 1885. Mrs. Knapp then went to Boston, but in 1888 returned to San Diego where she became an art teacher at the Southwest Institute, an exclusive private school at Fourth and Elm. Art, music, and literature were her interests. She was a talented writer and speaker, and an ardent advocate of women's rights. In 1885 while in Boston, she became a member of the Massachusetts Women's Suffrage Society. For the rest of her life she was active and prominent in the social and cultural life of San Diego.

In the first year of their marriage, Lydia Horton presided with grace over the mansion on First Street, during which time it saw more social activity than it had previously. On April 23, 1891, President and Mrs. Benjamin Harrison visited San Diego. They were driven in a parade on D Street and then up First Street to visit Mr. and Mrs. Horton.

His finances being such as they were, Horton was still interested in selling his home, but finding a buyer for such a large house was not easy. He advertised, not only locally, but in San Francisco and eastern papers. One advertisement read as follows:

"If you are thinking of a winter home in this most delightful of all resorts, I have to offer the finest estate in Florence Heights for sale at a very low figure, situated at First and Fir Streets, San Diego; is splendidly built, in thorough repair, fitted out with all modern conveniences such as both hot and cold water, pneumatic bells, etc.; occupying half a block of land, the house is surrounded by cement walks, garden and lawns. From its elevated position commands a view of ocean, bay, mountains, Pt. Loma, Coronado and city. Open for inspection every day from 1 to 3 p.m."

The house finally sold in 1892, and the Hortons then moved to 2829 State Street, in an eleven room, two story house built on the half block he had bought in Middletown. The house had an even more commanding view of the bay and Point Loma than did the house on First Street, but there was not much else in sight. It was the first, and for a long time the only house on the hill, which became known as "Horton Hill." Lumber and supplies to build the house were brought in by boat and landed at the foot of the hill, the bay coming up to what is now Pacific Highway.

The house was built with a veranda on three sides, east, south and west, and had the usual cupola and "widow's walk" on top. Horton, with his spy glasses, was always the first to spot a ship coming around Point Loma, and still had time to climb in his carriage, go down to Laurel, cross a bridge over what is now Reynard Way, then to Fifth and down to the wharf to greet the newcomers. Many a small child upon seeing him when first getting off

Fig. 92 "Father" Horton

the boat would shout to his parents, "Look, there's Santa Claus!" And Horton, with his long white beard, sparkling eyes, jolly smile and pink complexion, could well have been Santa Claus in mufti.

Loleta Levet Rowan, in her *Memoirs*, told about Horton and his State Street home:

"The view served a very real purpose in his life. With a pair of long range binoculars, he would scan the horizon for the first telltale wisp of smoke that would indicate a steamer was on the way. After sighting smoke, he would ride in haste to town and to the steamer landing. With his long flowing beard and dressed in black frock coat and black silk top hat, Horton was an impressive figure among the waiting townspeople. As a newcomer or tourist approached, Horton would grasp his hand and pat him on the back and sing out: "Well, well, well, what brings you to our beautiful San Diego?", and the passengers, having been carefully coached by the Captain of the ship, would reply, "Mr. Horton, you should know it was the bay and climate". And this was the cue for the ladies to applaud and the men to cheer and Horton to break into a grin. Horton loved his city and he was always immensely pleased to hear such complimentary remarks about it."

By 1890 the population of the city had leveled off to around 16,000, representing a fairly stable, permanent number of residents. Although this was a considerable drop from the height reached at the peak of the boom, it still was more than six times the population in the early eighties. Los Angeles, too, had suffered a tremendous decline in population, but still could boast of having 50,000 inhabitants.

San Diego had always maintained friendly relations with San Francisco, but there was bitter

Fig. 93   China painted by Lydia Horton

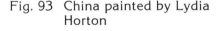

rivalry between Los Angeles and San Diego. Now, with the economy such as it was, and competition for new residents and industry being keen, Los Angeles bent every effort to keep newcomers from going to San Diego.

Traffic to California now was mostly by train, but San Diego had become only a branch out of Los Angeles. On all trains coming into Los Angeles, "runners" would hop aboard before its final destination and circulate among the passengers. Those who indicated an intention of going on to San Diego were then regaled with dire warnings—there was nothing in San Diego worth the trip, it was just a sleepy little Mexican village. When the passengers alighted at Los Angeles, the first thing they saw was a large poster, "advertising" San Diego. It showed a rutted street, a few shacks, and the only sign of life was a Mexican in a large sombrero leading a burro down the dusty road. The caption read, "San Diego on a busy day." To cap the insult, passengers for San Diego were warned there was no good drinking water in San Diego, and jugs of water were sold to those insisting on going on south. Many newcomers arrived clutching their jug of precious water.

Another reason for San Diego's slow growth was that some of its prominent and wealthy residents had come here to retire and did not want it to grow. One influential man was irate when he learned a streetcar line was to go past his home, disturbing his quiet neighborhood. He used all his power to delay this evidence of progress. There was no doubt about it, the "geranium growers" were in control.

Then John D. Spreckels came on the scene and really disturbed the serenity of the town. After taking over the Coronado Beach Company and south bay water developments, he purchased the *San Diego Union* in 1890, giving him a mouthpiece to the general public. The battle of the Spreckels' interests vs. the "geranium growers" was on in earnest, and would last for the next thirty years. Horton was never a "geranium grower." Spreckels arrived when Horton's influence had waned, and Horton must have watched with interest the growing conflict. It is a safe bet that he was in Spreckels' corner.

In 1890 the cable cars came to San Diego, but not for long. The ill-fated San Diego Cable Railroad was incorporated in 1889, not an auspicious year for such an undertaking. One of the incorporators was D.D. Dare, a partner in the California National Bank. A power house was built on the southwest corner of Fourth and Spruce, and a cable laid down

Fourth to C, then to Sixth, and down Sixth to the waterfront. On June 7, 1890, the first cable car, gaily decorated and carrying the San Diego Guard Band, ran on this route in a parade and ended at the power house where appropriate ceremonies were held. Mayor Douglas Gunn was speaker and Rose Hartwick Thorpe read one of her poems. Even Governor Waterman was present, honoring the occasion.

The little cable cars, described enthusiastically as "gorgeous little palaces on wheels," worked so well that the line was soon extended out Fourth to University Avenue, and then out Normal to "The Bluffs", overlooking Mission Valley. The first run to the Bluffs was on July 4, 1891, where a Pavilion had been built and a few trees planted on an otherwise barren cliff. This was the beginning of what became a little jewel of a park, known as Mission Cliff Gardens. It would later be developed under the watchful eye of John D. Spreckels. A Sunday afternoon ride on the cable car to the Pavilion became the thing to do. There were three turntables for the cable cars, one at the foot of Sixth, one at the power house, and another at the Pavilion. As in San Francisco, the passengers were glad to help the conductor turn the little car

Fig. 94   Cable car in front of the Florence Hotel

around. Unfortunately, the cable car company was declared insolvent in March, 1892, and shut down operations in October. It was fun while it lasted.

When the cable cars stopped running to the Bluffs, the street car which went out Fifth to University connected with a horse car carrying passengers to the Bluffs. A playground, with swings and a merry-go-round, was provided for the children. Sunday concerts were held at the Pavilion, which also became a popular place for dances, picnics and social functions.

In 1891 a Recreation Park was created on University Avenue. A grandstand, bleachers and board fence were erected. When the cable car company failed, and it became more difficult to reach the ball park, it was moved to Logan Heights.

The years 1891 to 1893 saw a series of bank crashes throughout the United States. There was a general financial depression everywhere, not just in Southern California. San Diego banks struggled

113

Fig. 95 Grey Stone "Castle" at Fifth
and Juniper

to keep their doors open and several were forced to close, never to reopen.

The first and most notorious of the San Diego bank failures was that of the California National Bank in 1891. This bank had been organized during the height of the boom in 1888 by J.W. Collins and D.D. Dare, two suave newcomers who were accepted into the community as respected citizens without any investigation into their past. Their bank was considered a sound one. In October,

1891, a sign went up that the bank was closed temporarily. A bank examiner was called in, and found that some $200,000 was missing. So was the co-owner, D.D. Dare, who it was learned, had left hastily for Europe. Collins did not get out of town fast enough. He was found and charged with embezzlement. The city jail was not considered plush enough for such a distinguished inmate, so he was allowed to stay in a room at the Brewster Hotel with a guard stationed outside his door. When Collins was informed he was to be taken to Los Angeles for incarceration, he asked to be excused, went into the bathroom and supposedly shot himself. A casket was brought in and the body hastily removed. It was afterward claimed that the "body" was not only still warm but very much alive, and that Collins, by this ruse, was able to get out of town to join his partner in Europe where they found the climate healthier.

It was largely due to the California National Bank failure that the cable railway was forced into receivership and its assets taken to secure its indebtedness to the bank. The receiver for the bank also took over the mansion of D.D. Dare, a huge grey stone "castle" at the corner of Fifth and Juniper, later sold to John H. Gay, owner of the Lakeside Hotel.

The Consolidated Bank of San Diego, a combination of the first two banks in San Diego, the Bank of San Diego and the Commercial Bank, and long considered as solid as the Rock of Gibraltar, was one of those to close in 1893. In this case it was more the result of the times, and possibly some mismanagement, but not because of fraud or dishonesty. The officers of the bank were highly respected, long time residents. Most of the old families of San Diego had savings in this bank and so were badly shaken. Fortunately, in the final settlement, the depositors received sixty-five percent of their money. The Consolidated Bank Building, at Fifth and G, was sold to Ralph Granger and later became the City Hall.

Of the eight banks in San Diego in 1889, five went out of business in the early nineties, leaving only the First National Bank, the Bank of Commerce and the San Diego Savings Bank. In the wave of bank failures many San Diegans saw their savings wiped out almost overnight. In spite of the depression, new businesses did come to San Diego, an evidence of faith in its future. The center of town was now moving up to Fifth and D.

In 1890 Adolph Levi opened a fine livery stable on the corner of Second and D, the Diamond Carriage and Livery Company, and advertised he would rent horses and carriages "with or without a driver." Upstairs was a large room which doubled as a roller skating rink and ballroom. The building was torn down in 1910 and became the site for the new Spreckels Theatre Building.

Also in 1890 Joseph Jessop opened his first jewelry store, on F between Fourth and Fifth. Jessop had left England in 1889 because of poor health. He brought his family to California, and decided to settle in San Diego.

In 1892 Matt Heller opened a "Cash Grocery" on the northwest corner of Eleventh and F, the start of a chain of "cash and carry" stores later absorbed into Safeway Stores.

One prominent business man who sold out and left town was Wyatt Earp.

The Chinese in the nineties still had a monopoly on the laundry business and in the fruit and vegetable market. However, customers watching the energetic Chinese doing their ironing were disconcerted by a certain habit observed among them, and reported their displeasure to the local health authorities. In 1898, at the insistence of the Health Inspector, the City Council passed an ordinance prohibiting laundry men from sprinkling clothes by "emitting water from the mouth." Four arrests were made and fines levied, although a lawyer for the defense pleaded the law was unconstitutional.

A Chinese fruit and vegetable vendor by the name of John Ling went each day to Coronado. One morning Ling, with his cart and faithful horse Pekin, was late to the ferry and just barely made it on board. The horse and cart were squeezed in at the back. When the steam whistle blew, it so frightened the nag it shoved back on its haunches, causing the cart to slip over the side, dragging the horse and Ling into the water. Soon Ling's head, along with heads of cabbages and lettuce, surfaced and he was pulled to safety by his queue. Pekin was not so fortunate. He and the cart sank to the bottom of the bay.

In 1892 another name was added to the list of distinguished men who were coming to San Diego to live, attracted by its climate, and confident in its future growth. This was U.S. Grant, Jr., son of the Civil War General and former President. He brought his attractive family to San Diego and purchased the three-story mansion at Eighth and Ash, built in 1888 by Ora Hubbell, a local banker. This mansion had a magnificent view and contained twenty-five rooms, a beautiful spiral staircase, stained glass windows and marble fireplaces. It was far more gorgeous than might be expected in a small town, and was considered entirely suitable for the son of an ex-President. Grant was soon involved in San Diego business and in 1895 purchased the Horton House.

With the Grants there came to San Diego, as governess for their children, Miss Anna Held. Miss Held came to the United States in 1869 from Germany where she was trained as a kindergarten teacher. While working as a governess in the East she met the famous English actress, Ellen Terry. They became close friends and Miss Held served as Miss Terry's traveling companion for a number of years. In 1891 she became governess for the Grant family. Soon after her arrival in San Diego she began buying land in La Jolla, and in 1894 started building small cottages on the hillside above the

Cove. Eleven cottages were built, and she called them the Green Dragon Colony. In the meantime, she married Max Heinrich, a singer and musician, and together they established the Green Dragon Colony as a cultural center, attracting artists, actors, musicians and writers. This Anna Held is not to be confused with the French actress of the same name, of "milk bath" fame. Anna Held Heinrich later sold her La Jolla property and went back to Germany, but left there when Hitler came to power. She died in London in 1942 at the age of ninety-four.

The year 1892 was an eventful one. January 12 saw the opening of San Diego's first really grand theatre, the Fisher Opera House, located on the east side of Fourth, between B and C. Built at a cost of $100,000 by John C. Fisher, and on money borrowed from the California National Bank, it was a thing of beauty, and said to be one of the finest theatres in the west. It was built of steel and brick, and Romanesque in style. The seating capacity was 1400, and the stage 70' x 43'. Its decor was ivory and gold, with red Brussels carpeting and red velvet seats, which soon became infested with fleas. There were elegant crystal chandeliers, and the boxes were lavish in gold paint and red velvet. The drop curtain was donated by the Ladies Annex of the Chamber of Commerce. The painted scene depicted the Plaza d'Erbe in Verona, showing a lively and colorful marketplace. The opening night's performance was by the Carleton Opera Company, and all the local notables were present, with the ladies in beautiful new dresses, depression or not.

John C. Fisher also was noted as the originator of the Floradora Girls, a sextette of San Diego girls, including Lolita Levet Rowan and Ada Bellou, later Mrs. Lyman J. Gage. The Floradora Girls became quite celebrated, traveling over the United States, and made a number of phonograph records. Fisher also managed Madame Helen Modjeska on one of her tours of the United States. When she appeared in San Diego at the Fisher Opera House, she said "It is the handsomest theatre in America." A more unprejudiced compliment was paid by Richard Mansfield who said, "I have seen plenty of houses, pretty in front, but never have I been in a theatre where every detail of convenience to the actor is so fully provided."

Many other famous personages trod the boards of Fisher Opera House. Mrs. Tom Thumb and her

Fig. 96 Madame Helen Modjeska

company of Lilliputians appeared there in 1892. She was the widow of General Tom Thumb, but was then married to Count Magri. She drove about town in the "smallest coach in the world," drawn by the "smallest horses in the world," driven by the "smallest coachman in the world."

Unfortunately, Fisher's Opera House was also a victim of the bank crash. John C. Fisher had been a partner with D.D. Dare in the cable railway and soon the theatre went into receivership. It was later sold to Madame Katherine Tingley who renamed it the Isis. It retained the same curtain with the colorful Verona scene, which audiences had become accustomed to, and the fleas, which still kept the audiences scratching.

In the midst of bank crashes, cable car failures and other depression problems, the townspeople took time out to celebrate. The city marked the 350th anniversary of Juan Rodríquez Cabrillo's discovery of the port with a three day ceremony and pageant depicting Cabrillo's landing. It was the brain child of Billy Carlson who conceived it as a publicity stunt to advertise San Diego. But the idea took hold and similar celebrations have been held each year since then, although not always under the auspices of the city.

The first Cabrillo Celebration was on September 28, 29, and 30, 1892. Engraved invitations were sent out by the Mayor, Matthew Sherman. Alonzo E. Horton was a member of the committee. The festivities were to open with Cabrillo arriving in a small ship representing the *San Salvador*. Manuel Cabral, a fisherman of La Playa, portrayed Cabrillo. He was decked out in a velvet suit, knee pants, and an ostrich plume in his hat. The ship was to land at the foot of D, near the Santa Fe station. The landing was timed to be at high tide. Unfortunately, there was a delay and by the time the *San Salvador* arrived, the tide had gone out and the boat got stuck 300 feet from dry land. The wooden wharf at the foot of D was only six feet wide and had a rickety handrail. When the crowd surged to the railing to welcome Cabrillo it gave way and many dignitaries, including the Mayor, fell into the bay, which at that point happened to be mud. Fortunately, only their pride was hurt. Cabrillo was then greeted on dry land by Indian chiefs. He unfurled the Spanish flag and "took possession" of the country in the name of the King of Spain. The party proceeded in a parade up D to the plaza where a triple arch of bunting and flowers extended across D Street. Several bands took part, including the local Guard band, the Army and Marine bands, and even one from Mexico City.

As a part of the celebration, there was an Indian Fiesta. Father Ubach brought to San Diego a group of Indians from San Luis Rey. A stockade was built for them on the block bounded by A, Ash, Third and Fourth. Their dancing and costumes, of paint and feathers, added to the color of the occasion, although some "costumes" turned out to be more paint than feather.

The three day event cost the city $5000, and at a time when money was hard to come by. The taxpayers must have questioned whether the publicity was worth that much of a cash outlay, but everyone had a grand time at the city's expense.

Also in 1892, Mount San Miguel, the mountain

Fig. 97   Mathew Sherman home,
Twenty-Second and Market
Streets

on which Horton took his "slide," was again in the news. A spring near the foot of the mountain had been discovered by Captain Charles Van Alen in 1887. He was fifty-eight and bald. He claimed that by drinking the spring water his hair had grown thick and auburn. A. H. Isham learned of this phenomenon and started bottling the water under the label "Waters of Life" and "Ponce de Leon's Elixir." He advertised:

"Not only does it restore hair on bald heads as luxuriantly as in youth, but we are told that the life giving powers of these waters does not rest with tresses. . . it promises to bring back youth. His Royal Highness, the Prince of Wales, has friends who examined the new growth effected (on Capt. Van Alen's head) with a view to the application of the waters to his own royal head, now bald."

Fig. 98 Ulysses S. Grant, Jr.
residence, Eighth and Ash

Bottles of this water were sent in carload lots to Boston and New York. This lucrative business came to an end, not by complaints of customers, but because Isham was sued for trespassing—it was somebody else's water he was bottling. Unfortunately, no one has tested scientifically the water from this spring, to prove or disprove its youth restoring propensities.

Another new industry developing in San Diego County was silk culture. In the days before synthetics, silk was a costly and treasured material. A "silk farm" was started in University Heights, near the Bluffs, and housewives were nursing silkworms in their backyards, confident that it would be a profitable venture. At the World's Fair in Chicago in 1893 San Diego County's Silk Exhibit was greatly admired and commented on. In fact, San Diego County was well represented at the fair. Its exhibits of a wide variety of fresh fruits won awards and gained recognition for San Diego County as a fruit growing community unsurpassed anywhere in the country.

In spite of the fact that real estate was in the doldrums, banks were failing right and left, and business in general had slackened, the city government in 1893 was rolling along with surprising momentum. Perhaps it should not be so surprising, when we remember that Mayor Billy Carlson was now at the helm. The City Treasurer in 1893 reported $809,000 in gold and $297,000 in silver in the city coffers, and this money was put to work in improving the city. In that year great strides were made in street paving and grading, something desperately needed. Now Fifth Street was paved from A to University Avenue, and then the road out University Avenue to La Mesa was graded. D was graded from Twenty-Fifth out to the El Cajon road. In March the Chamber of Commerce, with a concern for beauty, distributed 300 trees for street planting.

Also, by the early nineties, the San Diego Electric Company, successor to the Jenney Electric

Company, had laid twenty-nine miles of street lighting, including 150 arc lights and ten high towers. Houses had been wired over a radius of eight miles, with lights of sixteen candlepower.

In 1893 the Spreckels Company took over the street railway and converted it to electricity at a cost of $350,000, another evidence of John D. Spreckels' faith in San Diego. Just before, in December, 1892, the San Diego Railway Company had been warned against speeding. One of its horse cars had been seen going nineteen miles an hour on D. The maximum on the little cable cars had been ten miles an hour, down hill, and this was considered quite a fast clip.

The Spreckels Company saw the advantage of having an attraction at the end of a car line. The D Street line went to the top of the hill at 25th Street, where on the northwest corner was constructed a tower, known as the Observatory. It served as a waiting room, as well as a fine lookout over the city. Later, when the Spreckels Company acquired the Old Town Railway, "Ramona's Marriage Place" became the end of the line attraction. In 1898, the Spreckels Company took over the defunct cable car company, paying $19,000 for the track from the foot of Sixth to the Bluffs. Thrown in with the deal were the Pavilion, the twenty acres which became the Mission Cliff Gardens and also 450 lots in University Heights.

City Park, the huge 1400 acre tract laid out in 1869, was nothing more than a wasteland until the 1890s. It was inhabited by coyotes, rabbits, quail, lizards and snakes. A few Indians still camped on the mesa. It was also used by the city as a dump, for the disposal of refuse.

E. D. Switzer and his family lived on a farm where the city's Central Operational Center is now, on B between Nineteenth and Twentieth, giving the name Switzer to the canyon leading back of his farm. Also in Switzer Canyon, thought to be a safe distance from town, were some powder houses. On Sunday morning, September 29, 1895, the town was rocked by an explosion. One of the powder houses had blown up. It was believed to have been triggered by small boys playing in the canyon. North of Switzer, in the canyon, was a dairy. The City Pound was located in Cabrillo Canyon. This canyon had been known for its rattlesnakes. For obvious reasons, it was known as Rattlesnake Canyon, and later as Pound Canyon.

In 1890 the City Guard had its target range north of Pound Canyon, its firing platform being about where the Cabrillo Bridge is now. Until 1884 the range had been in Middletown, half way to Old Town. When traffic along this route became too heavy it moved to Rose Canyon, and then in 1890 to City Park, where they were sure it would never be disturbed by any population problem.

The first effort to beautify City Park was in 1889 when the Ladies Annex to the Chamber of Commerce raised $500 and planted a strip of trees along a ten acre stretch on the west side of the park, before Sixth Street was graded, and also a few trees along the edge of the park on Golden Hill.

Then in 1892 the city leased thirty acres at the northwest corner of City Park, at Sixth and Upas, to Kate O. Sessions for a nursery. As rent, she was to plant 100 trees each year in the park, and give the city an additional 300 trees. The first tree she planted was a cork, located about 300 yards from Upas Street. Miss Sessions introduced to San Diego the cork oak from Spain, camphor from Asia, rubber trees from the tropics, as well as the eucalyptus, acacia and a variety of other trees, local and foreign. She imported seeds from Australia, Asia, South America, Lower California, Spain and New England. Within a short time, her corner of the park had been changed from a wilderness to a place of beauty. Her bougainvillea, jasmine and acacia were especially admired. Her flower gardens extended to the bottom of the canyon, now Cabrillo Freeway. In 1903 she moved her nursery to Mission Hills, but in the eleven years she was in the park she planted many of the trees now so much admired, entitling her, without question, to be known as the "Mother of Balboa Park."

The lighthouse on Point Loma had long been a popular attraction for tourists, or for a Sunday picnic, even though it was not easy to get to. There were still few inhabitants, other than fishermen, on the point. Then the Federal Government, with some prodding by the Chamber of Commerce and by W.W. Bowers, now Congressman Bowers, began to take more interest in it.

In 1893 the Quarantine Station was completed, and later government coal bunkers were established. The lighthouse on the top of the hill was abandoned in 1891, and new ones built at the foot of the hill on the ocean side and on Ballast Point. This move was necessary because on foggy nights the ships could not see the light on top of the hill, or, when it was visible, it was frequently mistaken for a star. In 1896, when the war with Spain was threatening, the War Department began strengthening its defenses, and commenced fortifying Point Loma. San Diego then received its start as a military base. In 1899 Fort Rosecrans was named in honor of General William Rosecrans.

An interesting "character" on the San Diego scene in those days was Reuben the Guide. Some said he was a negro, others that he was Mexican. In either case, he dressed as a Mexican, with the large sombrero, serape and all the colorful trappings. He had a carriage for hire, and would meet the tourists as they arrived by train or ship. He did very well with his "One-half day Excursion to the Old Spanish Lighthouse." The "old" lighthouse on top of the hill had been built in 1854 by the United States government after California had become a state. It was never Spanish, nor even Mexican. However, the name sounded romantic and was good for business. Soon other guides were using the name, and even the old time residents found themselves referring to the "Old Spanish Lighthouse." The last Lighthouse Keeper on the top of the hill was Robert D. Israel, who served from 1871 to 1891. He and his family were always glad to greet the visitors who made the long trek out to the lighthouse.

San Diego was becoming more "cultural" in the nineties. In 1893 the Amphion Club was founded, its object being "to stimulate a higher degree of musical education among its members and also to elevate the musical taste of the community." Originally, it provided an audience to aspiring young San Diego musicians, but later brought great musical artists to San Diego. For years it was under the capable direction of Misses Gertrude and Bess Gilbert and Mrs. B.A. Buker. Under its auspices, all the world's greatest musicians appeared in San Diego—at the Fisher Opera House and later at the Spreckels Theatre. The Wednesday Club was organized in 1895, as a literary and cultural club. It met in a cottage on Pennsylvania Avenue across from All Saints Episcopal Church. Mrs. Alonzo E. Horton was its first President. In 1911 it built its present club house at Sixth and Ivy Lane.

In 1895 the Chamber of Commerce reported the main industries of San Diego County to be fruit growing, mining (Julian), honey (producing one to two million pounds a year), and fishing. In the same year, great excitement prevailed when an oil well was drilled on Point Loma. The populace was assured there was oil. Everyone with a few dollars wanted to get in on the speculation. But as so often, it turned out to be nothing but high hopes.

While the excitement lasted, however, there arrived one of the most interesting personalities ever to establish residence in San Diego, Madame Katherine A. Tingley. With one eye on the posibility of oil being discovered on her land, but with the

Fig. 99 Robert D. Israel

121

Fig. 100   Katherine A. Tingley

Loma an "Arabian Nights" atmosphere. Persons seeing the buildings for the first time must have rubbed their eyes in astonishment and disbelief—were they *real*?

Among the exotic buildings were the Isis Conservatory of Music and Drama, the "Lotus Home" for refugee Cuban children, the Raja Yoga Academy and the exquisite glass-domed Temple of Peace. A beautiful Greek Theatre was built on a site directly overlooking the Pacific Ocean. The buildings were all white, giving it the name of The White City. There were eventually a total of fifty buildings on the grounds.

The school was described as "a temple of living light, lighting up the dark places of the earth. . .the children will be taught the laws of physical, moral and mental health, and spiritual unfoldment. They will learn to live in harmony with nature. . .they will grow strong in an understanding of themselves and as they gain strength they will learn to use it for the good of the whole world." The doctrine of the movement was a hope for a better life through exemplary living and a search for great truth from past ages, coupled with a belief in Spiritualism and Reincarnation.

Followers of Madame Tingley were called Tingleyites. Many persons of wealth were attracted to the movement, the most prominent perhaps being A.B. Spalding the sporting goods "king," who was one of her converts and built a home on the grounds. Those who came to live in the community were expected to turn over their wealth to her and live in an Utopian society where everyone would receive according to his needs. Everyone was given a job, from the menial to the highly accomplished. There was no doubt about it, Madame Tingley had a way about her. Her magnetism drew people from all walks of life to her door. She was especially adept as a fund raiser and "converting" men of wealth to her cause. She attracted famous artists and musicians, some of whom came to live at The Homestead, others to perform in the Greek Theatre, or at the Isis Theatre. She brought to San Diego and to Southern California a "culture" never dreamed of before and a "mystique" never known again.

The settlement on the Point became a great tourist attraction and has been described as the most magnificent of all the Utopian societies of the nineteenth century. It was frankly an "escapist" society, an attempt to live in a dream world apart from all the trouble, stress and strain of an emerging industrial society.

Madame Tingley was a demanding leader. Soon

other on the beauty of the location, in 1896 she purchased 130 acres on Point Loma for the purpose of establishing a school for "the Revival of the Lost Mysteries of Antiquity," and to teach the esoteric lore of the East.

On February 24, 1897, the cornerstone was laid for the first building, The School of Antiquity. The Mayor and some one thousand San Diego residents trekked out the seventeen miles to Point Loma in a procession of buggies to attend the event.

The name Katherine A. Tingley was already well known among Theosophists the world over. She was the leader of a contingent of dissidents who desired to break away from the main organization of the Theosophist Society, whose headquarters were in Boston, and to establish a new branch of the society.

In 1898 the Universal Brotherhood & Theosophical Society was formed and in 1900 Point Loma became its international headquarters. Students, disciples and followers came from all over the world. Buildings were erected which gave Point

there began rumblings and whispers about the goings on in the White City. It was said the guards who patrolled the grounds were armed, and that no one could leave without the leader's permission. Disgruntled members who did leave were glad, even anxious, to give interviews to newspaper reporters. Curiosity was great on the part of readers anxious for every morsel of gossip. Some scandalous stories were told. Some may have been true, others most likely were more the creation of a fertile imagination than fact. To add fuel to the fire, Madame Tingley was frequently involved in lawsuits, which made for interesting newspaper reading.

In 1899 the *Los Angeles Times*, whose editor was Harrison Gray Otis, intimated that Madame Tingley had converted to her own use funds collected for destitute Cubans, and there was other improper conduct on The Homestead. Finally Madame Tingley filed a libel suit. Judge W.R. Andrews represented her. The *Times* was represented by Samuel Shortridge, later United States Senator from California. From the beginning it appeared the *Times* would lose. It was just a question of the amount of damages. The *Times* attempted to introduce evidence of Madame Tingley's spiritualistic activities in Massachusetts under her maiden name of Kitty Westcott. Judge Torrance ruled this evidence inadmissable. He said what was to be determined was whether or not the Point Loma institution was "a place of horrors" where inmates did not get enough to eat, were given inade-

Fig. 101 The Homestead, Point Loma

Fig. 102 Greek Theatre

quate shelter and forcibly restrained from their "liberty." Shortridge in an eloquent speech said "No despot that sat in Constantinople ever claimed to exercise such powers over men and women as Mrs. Tingley does."

Crowds showed up for the trial. It was better than an expensive show at the Fisher Opera House, especially the repartee between Shortridge and Tingley. The case dragged on, but finally in January, 1903, Madame Tingley was declared the winner and the court awarded her $7500.00 in damages. Otis and the *Times* were relieved; it could have been much worse.

In another spicy courtroom trial, Tingley was charged with alienating the affections of the wealthy husband of the plaintiff. (Actually it was for alienating his money.) This case Tingley lost, and paid off. Madame Tingley's favorite color was purple, giving her another title, "The Purple Mother." She rode about San Diego in an open carriage, and later in one of the first large open autos. She always sat in the center of the back seat, on a raised seat or dais, so she appeared to be on a throne. Anyone accompanying her had to ride backward, facing her.

Her name also caused some confusion. Some sailors whose ship was coming into the bay, and who were looking forward to a night on the town, meaning in the Stingaree, were shown the beautiful white buildings on Point Loma and told "That is Madame Tingley's place." One sailor, unfamiliar with San Diego, admitted the Madam must run a pretty fancy establishment, but wanted to know "Why is her place so far from town?"

The fortunes of Madame Tingley and her White City gradually diminished as the new century and a new era came into being. In 1929 she died at the age of eighty-two. In 1942 The Homestead was closed down. After World War II the property became the site of California Western University, and now Point Loma College. One of the few evidences that remains of the dream world that once existed there is the Greek Theatre, still a focal point beside the blue Pacific.

Another resident whose accomplishments on behalf of San Diego are all but forgotten was Harr Wagner, a boomtime arrival, founder of the ill-fated College of Letters at Pacific Beach, an educator and book publisher. Wagner's abilities were recognized sufficiently to warrant his appointment as Superintendent of Schools of San Diego in 1889, in which office he served until 1895. When his dreams of a private college collapsed with the boom, he then concentrated his efforts on getting the state to establish a Normal School in the area. He was supported enthusiastically by the citizens of San Diego who found it costly to send their children away from home for their college education. The movement to establish a Normal School began in earnest in 1894 while Wagner was Superintendent of Schools. In 1895 a bill passed the state legislature authorizing the Normal School, but was vetoed by the Governor. Finally, in 1897, it passed again and became the law.

In 1898, Samuel T. Black, then State Superintendent of Public Instruction, was named the first President. There were ninety-three students in the first class, which met in rooms in the Hill Block at Sixth and F. This was on the site of Horton's Hall which burned in 1897. Horton had long since disposed of this property. The new owner built a new and modern building in its place. On opening day, November 1, 1898, President Black said, "No other Normal School had so auspicious an opening." This, in spite of the fact that attendance was low on that first day, because there was a circus in town which the students did not want to miss.

The Normal Schools were established and maintained by the state for the purpose of training young men and women to be teachers in its public schools. Furthermore, those accepted as students were required to sign an agreement to teach upon completion of their studies. It is interesting to note that each morning before commencement of classes, the students joined together in saying the

Lord's Prayer and the reading of scriptures.

Three sites were proposed for the new Normal School. The buildings and grounds of the old College of Letters at Pacific Beach were offered. A value of $100,000 was placed on them. This site had the enthusiastic support of San Diegans and the Chamber of Commerce. Escondido offered its three-story high school and grounds, as a possible site. Then the College Hill Land Association, composed of promoters of the University Heights development, offered the State eleven acres in University Heights at Normal and El Cajon Boulevard. A Board appointed by the Governor selected the University Heights site.

A beautiful white building, with Doric columns, was designed. The cornerstone was laid December 10, 1898, and the building dedicated May 1, 1899. Horton was one of the honored guests at the dedication, and congratulated the students.

The establishment of a college in University Heights gave a great boost to that area. The residential population was already moving in that direction. In the mid-nineties a Grammar School was opened at University and Vermont, known as the University Heights School.

Then in 1897 the San Diego Country Club was organized, the first golf club in San Diego. The University Heights Land Company donated land near Upas and Park Boulevard, and a small club house was built. There were no "greens," only

Fig. 103 State Normal School,
Normal and El Cajon
Boulevard

Fig. 104   San Diego Country Club
near Park Boulevard and
Upas

brown dirt and plenty of sand and weed traps. The nine hole course was on City Park land and extended to where the Natural History Museum is now. When the alfalfa and rye grew so high the balls were lost, members gathered with scythes to cut the weeds. Then someone hit on the idea of letting Charles Hardy run sheep from his slaughter house pens to do the job. On the second day, they were rounded up and impounded by the Poundmaster, the Pound being in the canyon just to the south. It took a bit of political maneuvering before the sheep were released and allowed to finish the job. In 1913 the club moved to Point Loma and in 1920 to its present location in Chula Vista.

The year 1896, in October, saw the opening of "Marston's Folly," San Diego's first really large department store. The dry goods store of George W. Marston had been located for years at the cor-

ner of Fifth and F. Then his uncle, Stephen W. Marston, of Boston, purchased two lots on the southwest corner of Fifth and C, and constructed for his nephew a four-story building, built around an open court, and boasting both an elevator and electric lights. Because the building was so far up town, and so big for so little a town, it was called "Marston's Folly."

Nevertheless, within a few years it was outgrown and George W. Marston purchased all the lots on the north side of C, between Fifth and Sixth, and constructed a new five-story building. The new store opened in 1912 under the name of The Marston Company. For nearly fifty years after that, Marston's continued to be *the* place to shop in San Diego. The name carried a prestige and guarantee of quality of merchandise no other store could quite meet.

In 1938, on the occasion of the store's Sixtieth Anniversary, George W. Marston was quoted: "We have resisted becoming part of a chain store no matter how important the chain. We want to remain just Marston's and jog on in good old San Diego style for another 60 years or so."

Alas, "Marston's" would be a household word only for the next twenty years, then it would fall victim to the times and merge with the Broadway Department Stores. Marston's store is now only a nostalgic memory, as is Hamiltons's, the fine grocery store established in the 1870s by his former partner.

One of the most significant events of the 1890s was the purchase by the city of Horton's Plaza, the half block on D between Third and Fourth, across the street from the Horton House, and shown on all city maps as a plaza. No taxes had ever been assessed on the property.

To make sure that San Diego would always have a "plaza" on that spot, Horton had made the following statement, or "reservation:"

San Diego, Cal. June 20, 1871
This may certify that I, A.E. Horton, San Diego, Cal. do hereby agree to keep that part of Block 42 in Horton's Addition to San Diego bounded by the south line of D Street for 200 feet in width from east to west and 145 feet from north to south, open and free from buildings for any purpose whatever and to keep the same as a Plaza as represented to the parties purchasing property on the remainder of said Block 42.

This document was not recorded until July 13, 1882.

The plaza originally extended the full half block to the adjoining property. Then an "alley" or street

Fig. 105 Marston's Store, Fifth and F

was created and given the name Witherby Street, in honor of Judge Oliver S. Witherby, a District Judge in the early 1850s. Horton had built a fountain and planted a hedge around the square. Later a bandstand was erected where the City Guard Band gave a concert once a week on Saturday nights. There were only a few benches, so the people just strolled around listening to the concert and chatting with their friends. For a while the band was paid $50 a month by the city. Then, when the city was criticized for this expenditure, it was continued by public subscription.

By 1890 the plaza had become dirty and unsightly and the city began to wonder what should be done about it. The question of title and ownership was raised, and Horton's Reservation of June 20, 1871 came to light.

On August 30, 1890, Horton wrote to the Board of Public Works of the City of San Diego as follows:

Gentlemen:
Responding to your letter of the 28th instant, requesting me to state the purposes for which the Horton Plaza was set apart for public use and my desires in respect to its improvement. . . The present so called park should be condemned and removed—hedge, trees, fountain, bandstand and all. Instead of being an attractive and useful place, it is unsightly, a receptacle for dust and filth and a hiding place for vice.

My object in dedicating the grounds to the public use was mainly to provide a central, commodious and attractive place for public meetings, public announcements, public recreation, and for any other proper public purpose; a place where all public questions might be discussed with comfort, where public open air concerts might be given, where the people might rest, and where children might play in safety.

He then went on to make certain suggestions:
Around the 3rd, 4th and D Street margins circular places should be provided in which trees should be planted in double rows and far enough apart to not obstruct view.

Each tree should be enclosed by a circular seat of iron, so small that a toper could not recline on it, and having a high back formed to protect the tree.

Very truly yours,
A.E. Horton

In 1892 the City Attorney informed the city that it had no right to construct any improvements on the plaza which would interfere with its use as a plaza, as it was so designated by Horton's Reserva-

Fig. 106 Bandstand in the plaza

tion. It was then suggested that the city should buy Horton's interest, whatever it was, reversionary or otherwise.

By this time, Horton's finances were precarious. He had disposed of most of his properties and his income was very little, and he was an old man. He was glad of an opportunity to pick up some unexpected money. The city thought this would be a fine way to help him out financially, at a time when there was no such thing as Social Security, and charity was an unpleasant word. So negotiations were started to buy this half block. Horton claimed he had been offered as much as $50,000 for it, but he had refused all offers, preferring it to remain for public use. He then offered to sell his interests to the city for $10,000, payable $100 a month, without interest. In this way, he believed he would

be assured a life income. On November 7, 1894, a deed was executed to the city, which read in part as follows:

". . . in consideration of the payment to A.E. Horton of the sum of $100 on the 1st day of each month, beginning 1st day of January 1895, and continuing during the lifetime of said A.E. Horton, provided no greater amount than $10,000 in the aggregate shall be paid, and in the event of the death of said A.E. Horton before the said aggregate amount of $10,000 shall have been paid, then all payments shall cease, and the obligation on the part of the city of San Diego to make further payments shall become null and void . . ."

The city was pleased with this deal. Horton was then eighty-one years of age and the chance he would live to receive the full $10,000 seemed remote. The city was willing to gamble that it would acquire the title to the plaza for a good deal less than $10,000. But on this wager the city lost. Payments of $100 per month commenced, in accordance with the deed, on January 1, 1895 and continued to April, 1903 when the full $10,000 had been paid. Horton was then eighty-nine years old and still going strong!

Chapter Fourteen

The Dawn of a New Era, 1900–09

The new century dawned without much fanfare in San Diego. It did, however, bring new hope for the future. The population during the past ten years had remained almost static. There were now approximately 17,000 residents, representing a gain of only about 1,000 in ten years. However, the next six years would see the population double, due in large measure to a new breed of business men who were arriving. In addition to Spreckels, they included Louis J. Wilde, D.C. Collier, O.W. Cotton and Ed Fletcher, to name a few. They were the City Builders who took over the helm and built on the foundation Horton had laid.

The Spreckels' interests were in control of water developments, transportation and the *San Diego Union*. In 1895 the *Evening Tribune* came into existence, in opposition to the *Union* and to Spreckels. Its owners were intent on fighting Spreckels and his Southern California Mountain Water Company. After considerable litigation, the lawsuits were settled, and then Spreckels bought out the *Tribune* in 1901. His newspaper opponent now was E.W. Scripps, self-styled "Damned Old Crank," and owner of the *Sun*, who for years would be one of Spreckels' most vocal critics. Spreckels then bought the old Horton "Bank" Building at Third and D for $10,000 and moved his newspapers to that building. This forced the city to find a new location for its City Hall.

The old Consolidated Bank Building at Fifth and G was leased from Ralph Granger and converted into a City Hall. There the city remained until the new Civic Center on the waterfront was built in the 1930s.

San Diegans now, thanks to Spreckels, had a new summer resort, Tent City, opened in 1901 on the Strand below the Hotel del Coronado. San Diegans old enough to remember Tent City do so with nostalgia—especially the exhilarating ferry ride, and the rush to get a side seat in the open street cars that carried passengers from the ferry to the end of Tent City. On each side of the streetcar tracks were rows of tent cottages, some covered with thatch. In even the best, the floors were hard, the furniture sparse and old. Light was provided by a naked globe hanging down the middle of the room. Each tent was supplied with a washstand and a pitcher for water. Those were still the days of the "Chic Sale," so it was not considered an inconvenience to have to walk to "facilities." The only privacy afforded in the tent was a curtain which could be drawn to partition it into two rooms. But in the days before there was an automobile in every garage, all this was an exciting experience and one to be remembered for all time. If accommodations left a lot to be desired (from the present point of view) the entertainment provided was far beyond what the average family ever expected to experience.

Boardwalks extended down the strand on both the bay and ocean sides of Tent City. Just below the hotel was an enclosed salt water plunge. An open children's pool, 100' x 175' in size, was farther down on the bay side and was affectionately known as "John D. Spreckels' Bathtub." At the deep end it was only three and one half feet, but the *piece de resistance* was the slide which plummeted the youngsters into the water with a splash, bottom first. The more timid required a push from behind to get started, but after the first slide went eagerly back for more.

On the bay, in an area roped off for the experienced swimmers, were a float and some diving boards. Non-swimmers could stand along the boardwalk and watch the divers in their fancy high dives. On the ocean side, there was an Arcade building, with a Curio Shop decorated with bright Japanese lanterns, a cafeteria and a grocery store. On the bay side was a classier cafe. Few of those occupying the tents ever indulged in a meal at the Hotel del Coronado. That was only for the very rich. Some did venture into the lobby to admire the plush furnishings and gaze in admiration at the fabulous Crown Room. They might sit a few minutes in a rocking chair on the veranda, but then would return to Tent City where they were more at home. Here were two worlds, face to face, each enjoying the other from a distance, and, presumably, without much envy.

The ferry *Silver Gate* had been converted into a dance pavilion. When it sank, a new dance hall was built. Also on the bay side was an open air bandstand. Spreckels brought to Coronado from Honolulu a bandmaster, Henry Ohlmayer, whose band provided free concerts. The music was mostly that of Strauss and Souza, familiar melodies and stirring marches.

After World War I and the advent of the automobile Tent City went into a decline. By 1941 it had become only a memory. San Diegans were now traveling farther afield for their vacations. Looking back, one wonders how all that canvas and those thatched roofs escaped a conflagration which should have ended Tent City long before.

In 1902 San Diego acquired its first library building. After its first home in the Consolidated Bank Building, the library moved to the Express Building. Then in 1893 it moved to new and larger quarters in the St. James Hotel Annex, directly over the Post Office. Five years later it moved again to the Keating Building, Fifth and F. At this

Fig. 107 Tent City, Coronado

time, the Secretary of the Library Board was Mrs. A.E. Horton. In June of 1899 she wrote Andrew Carnegie, who was then endowing libraries all over the United States, and told him of San Diego's need. Her letter brought a prompt reply:

Skibo Castle, Ardgay, N.B.
7th July 1899

Mrs. A.E. Horton
Free Public Library, San Diego, Cal.
Madam:
   If the city were to pledge itself to maintain a free public library from taxes, say to the extent of the amount you name, of between five and six thousand dollars a year, and provide a site, I shall be glad to give you $50,000 to erect a suitable library building.
Very truly yours,
Andrew Carnegie

Great was the jubilation among the local citizenry to whom a library meant so much. But then there arose the inevitable controversy over a site. Several locations were suggested, each bringing forth supporters and opponents. Finally, the city agreed to pay $17,000 for the half block on E between Eighth and Ninth.

The cornerstone was laid March 19, 1901. Judge M.A. Luce was the speaker and Mrs. Horton read a paper giving the history of the library. The architects chosen were Ackerman & Ross of New York, designers of the Congressional Library in Washington, D.C. The building was completed and opened in April, 1902. George W. Marston paid for the landscaping, employing Miss Kate O. Sessions who planted rare specimens of palm trees around the beautiful building.

The Carnegie grant of $50,000, with an additional $10,000 added later, was the first made to a California city. But because of the delay over selection of a site, the Oakland Library was the first completed.

Also in 1902 the vast wasteland that was City Park finally got some attention. In that year the Chamber of Commerce formed a Park Improvement Committee, appointing as members Julius Wangenheim, George W. Marston, U.S. Grant, Jr., D.F. Garrettson, and William Clayton. Later Kate O. Sessions was named to the committee, probably the first woman to serve on any committee of that august male body.

The committee, with Julius Wangenheim as Chairman, proposed that a beginning be made at Sixth and Date, the southwest corner and the highest point in the park, from which there was a magnificent view. This point was known as Lookout Point, and in 1924 was renamed Marston Point, in honor of the great contribution of George W. Marston to the park development.

From 1902 to 1905 committee members used their own funds in aid of the park. Other individuals and organizations contributed funds to purchase trees. The suggested park improvement met with the enthusiastic support of all San Diegans. On July 4, 1903, members of the Woodmen of the World celebrated with a parade, ending at the park where 1000 trees, mostly eucalyptus, were planted in Pound Canyon. On Arbor Day in 1904 more than 4000 adults and 2000 school children turned out for a massive tree planting along Sixth and down into Pound Canyon (now Cabrillo Freeway.)

George W. Marston, at a personal cost of $10,000, brought to San Diego Samuel Parsons, Jr., of New York, President of the American Society of Landscape Architects, who was requested to submit a plan for park improvements. He arrived in San Diego in December, 1902. Parsons is credited with the first long range planning for park improvement. Work commenced under his plan in March, 1903, at the southwest corner of the park.

The Chamber of Commerce then brought to San Diego as Secretary of the Park Improvement Committee, Mrs. Mary B. Coulston, who previously was editor of the magazine *Garden and Forest*, in New York City. She was a dynamic person and a fine speaker. She was often called upon to make talks about the park plans, and was a frequent contributor to newspapers and periodicals of articles concerning the park. Unfortunately, she died suddenly on July 16, 1904, while in Berkeley. This came as a great shock to her many friends in San Diego where she had endeared herself in the short time she had been here. Memorial services were held in Unity Hall (on Sixth, between B and C). Members of the Wednesday Club were in charge. William E. Smythe was Chairman of the occasion. Later, her cremated remains were strewn under a tree in her beloved City Park.

In 1903 grading began on Sixth Street along the Park. The extension of Sixth to University Avenue was then called Park Avenue. In some of the old sidewalks along Sixth, one can still see the name "Park Ave." engraved in the cement. The name was not changed to Sixth until just before the 1915 Exposition, when Park Boulevard was cut through from Twelfth Street. At that time there was a hue and cry because the new Park Boulevard would

Fig. 108 San Diego's Carnegie
Library

destroy some palm trees and natural rock formations in that area.

There was much opposition also to putting a
street along the park, on Sixth, but the park planners won out. One suggestion that fortunately was
not carried out, was that Pound Canyon (Cabrillo)
should be filled with water making a lake. It was to
be stocked with fish and filled with water lilies. Par-
sons vetoed this plan, saying it would become a
stench hole.

At the same time that work started at Sixth and
Date, Matt Heller and other residents of Golden Hill
began some improvements at the Twenty-Fifth
Street entrances to the park, including a children's
playground, where swings were set up, sand and
sawdust brought in, and trees that would make for
good climbing were planted. This was the begin-

ning of what became known as Golden Hill Park, a
part of City Park.

In 1905 the City Charter was amended to provide
an annual park appropriation, and the city then for
the first time assessed taxes for park development.
In April, the city appointed a Board of Park Commissioners, who would take over the responsibility
formerly borne by the Chamber of Commerce.

While the Chamber of Commerce and the city
were concerned with City Park, John D. Spreckels
was busy improving Mission Cliff Park, later
known as Mission Cliff Gardens, the exquisite little
park on the bluffs overlooking Mission Valley. The
gardens were owned and operated by the San
Diego Electric Railway and were free to the public.
In 1904 the company employed John Davidson, a
landscape gardener, to landscape and improve the
park. Davidson, a native of Scotland, where he
received his training, had recently been employed
by the Coronado Beach Company. He moved with
his family to the Pavilion in the park. One of his

Fig. 109 The Pavilion, Mission Cliff Gardens

first projects was to supervise the construction of the stone wall around the park, a work of art, which still remains, extending on Adams Avenue from Park Boulevard west to the canyon. He then landscaped the grounds with palms, eucalyptus, cypress, acacia and cedar trees. Paths were laid out with benches and pergolas at view spots where one could sit and look at the peaceful valley below, with its truck gardens laid out like giant checkerboards. Just below was a dairy from where the mooing of the cows could be heard in the stillness. Occasionally, a horse drawn vehicle would be seen plodding along the dusty road. In time of flood, all of San Diego rushed to the gardens to watch the flow of the water, sometimes from bank to bank.

Also in the park was an aviary, with every kind of bird imaginable. Especially popular were the talking parrots. Many valuable birds were donated by families who could no longer care for their pets. Parrots were frequently given, but first had to be kept in isolation until their vocabulary had been

approved. At the east end was a deer park and pheasant farm. Just to the east of the entrance was the Ostrich Farm, which had first been in Coronado and then moved to Mission Cliff Gardens. The Ostrich Farm extended from Park Boulevard east to the car barns on Florida Street. It was the only concession in the park to which there was an admission charged. Inside, one could watch the ostriches being ridden by the trainers or buy a huge ostrich egg (filled or blown). Popular with the ladies were the ostrich plumes, bought to adorn their hats. For those who did not want to spend the money or take the time to go in the Ostrich Farm, the board fence along Adams Avenue was full of knot holes and children and adults alike could always find one at eye level. If one were lucky, he could see the ostriches being ridden, or just see

133

one with its head "buried" in the sand.

The flower gardens, tended lovingly by Davidson and his helpers, were a sight to behold, especially the Easter lilies when they were all in bloom. Spreckels was especially fond of this park and would personally walk through it with Davidson, and make plans for new gardens and improvements. It was Spreckels' intention to build an outdoor organ at a location in the park overlooking the valley. Then came the plans for an exposition. The organ he had visualized for Mission Cliff Gardens was given to Balboa Park.

Until the exposition and the development of Balboa Park, Mission Cliff Gardens was the only real park in the city. It was easily accessible, and on Sunday the whole family could climb aboard a streetcar and go to the Gardens. For years there was a jolly conductor on the Fifth Street carline. On Sunday morning, when the streetcar stopped at Fifth and Pennsylvania to let off those going to All Saints Episcopal Church, he would call out: "All the saints off here. The sinners go on with me to Mission Cliff Gardens."

Again it was the advent of the automobile that

Fig. 110 Horton and "Dolly" in front of the Bayview Hotel

caused the demise of Mission Cliff Gardens. People were now taking Sunday drives in their autos instead of riding the streetcar to the Pavilion. The gardens were maintained until after Spreckels' death, but were finally closed in 1929 and the land subdivided into residential lots.

Soon after the turn of the century there was a surprising growth in population and a spurt of new business building, the first since the boom. One of the first of the new buildings promised was a large hotel to replace the old Horton House, now owned by U.S. Grant, Jr. The new hotel would be named the U.S. Grant, as a memorial to his father.

On the evening of July 12, 1905, a large crowd assembled at the Horton House for a ceremony to remove the first bricks before it was demolished. Father Horton, at age ninety-one, was the guest of honor and asked to remove the first brick, and after him, E.W. Morse and W.W. Bowers, all of whom had been present at the laying of the cornerstone of the Horton House thirty-five years before. Bowers, former Congressman, who had done so much to bring recognition to San Diego, was the principal speaker. He said: "It is such men as Horton and Morse that build cities. Natural advantages or beauty of situation never built a city...Old Horton House, right well have you fulfilled the promise...It is with feelings tinged with real sorrow that your creator and builders are now compelled to say to you, 'Old House, goodbye, goodbye'."

Horton, in a little speech, said he was not sorry to see his hotel go, for in its place would be erected an even finer edifice, a tribute to his growing city. It was at this time he told his friends gathered around him that he rejoiced more in his title "Father" than he would the title of President of the United States. Cheers went up for Horton and for the old Horton House which had played such an important part in the development of the city. The City Guard Band was on hand for the occasion, and at the conclusion of the ceremony, fireworks were shot into the sky.

A week before, at an auction of the furnishings of the Horton House, Horton bought a hair sofa, two rocking chairs and a writing desk. He said he wanted to be the first to register and stay in the new hotel when it was completed. Unfortunately, financial troubles prevented the prompt completion of the hotel and it was not opened until after his death.

A few days after the ceremony marking the demolition of the Horton House, San Diegans were shaken by the explosion of the gunboat Bennington

Fig. 111   Burial of the victims from the *Bennington* explosion

in the harbor. On the morning of July 21, as the *Bennington* lay at anchor just off the Santa Fe wharf, its boilers burst, killing fifty-one outright, nine died later, and forty-six were injured. Most of those who died were buried at Fort Rosecrans Military Cemetery. In January, 1908, the Bennington Monument at Fort Rosecrans was dedicated in memory of those lost in this holocaust.

During its early years, San Diego had been known as a "One Man Town,"—Horton's. For the first twenty years of the new century, it would again be known as a "One Man Town," belonging to John D. Spreckels. Spreckels, as Horton had been before, was in turn criticized, vilified and admired. In retrospect, one can only be grateful to them. San Diego was fortunate in having these two men in its early development. Without them, its history might have been very different.

After rescuing Coronado and the south bay from financial disaster, and taking over and providing essential local transportation important to the expansion and growth of the community, Spreckels finally became a resident of Coronado. He would now devote all his energies to the development of Coronado and San Diego. For years he complained of San Diego's "peanut politicians" who warned of "crafty schemes of Spreckels," their failure to cooperate with him, and of their petty jealousies.

Fig. 112 George W. Marston

He stated forthrightly that he was a businessman, not a Santa Claus. He was building San Diego to make his investments pay, not to make himself a dictator. He loved San Diego and believed in its future. His sole aim was to build it into a great city. He encouraged other big money interests to come to San Diego, but most went to Los Angeles where the local politicians recognized the need for them and pulled together. In San Diego, according to Spreckels, there was a continual tug of war between various political factions.

Until 1906, Spreckels had maintained his home in San Francisco, traveling back and forth between there and Coronado on his luxury yacht. Early 1906 found him seriously ill, so ill in fact that his death was actually expected by his family. Then, in April came the San Francisco earthquake and fire. Out of necessity, he and his family fled on their yacht to Coronado and to the Hotel del Coronado. His health immediately took a turn for the better, and within a few months he was fully recovered and taking an active part in his San Diego business ventures. He started construction of a home in Coronado, across from the hotel, completed at a cost of more than $100,000. Included in the construction was a fine pipe organ. He also built and donated to Coronado a library. He then began acquiring property in San Diego. At one time he owned all the lots on the south side of D from the Santa Fe Station to the Plaza.

In 1906 the old Horton Bank Building, which then housed the offices of the *Union* and *Tribune*, was torn down. A new Union Building was constructed. Completed in 1907, it became the first of several office buildings built by Spreckels. In 1912 he would build the Spreckels Theatre and office building. The theatre, which opened on August 23, 1912, was considered one of the largest and most beautiful in the country. He built the San Diego Hotel, and had under construction at the time of his death the new Spreckels Building (now Bank of America Building at Sixth and Broadway). The Golden West Hotel, at Fourth and G, Spreckels built as a workingman's hotel, for those who could not afford his San Diego Hotel or the U.S. Grant Hotel. He wanted to be known as the "Builder of San Diego." He was accused by the "geranium growers" of being for "smokestacks" whereas actually he was for both commercial interests and beauty. That is evident by his promotion of the beauty of Coronado, and Mission Cliff Gardens.

At one time Spreckels offered to build a new courthouse for the city, on his block across the street from its then location, but the city officials

Fig. 113 Coronado Home of John D. Spreckels

turned it down. If the politicians did not approve of Spreckels, the people did. When Spreckels wanted the City Charter to be amended to extend his streetcar line franchise from twenty-five to fifty years, so he could expand and improve the service, the politicians fought him tooth and nail, but the vote of the people was two to one in his favor.

Spreckels and the Spreckels Companies were estimated at one time to be paying ten percent of all city and county taxes. Only the people realized that Spreckels' prosperity was their prosperity and that San Diego was lucky to have him.

On December 14, 1906, only a few months after Spreckels had moved to Coronado, the *San Diego Union* came out with this headline: "RAILROAD FROM SAN DIEGO TO YUMA IS NOW ASSURED." Spreckels had announced his intention of building the railroad himself, and incorporated the San

Diego & Arizona Railroad for this purpose. Regardless of what politicians thought of him, Spreckels' word was good. The news was received with cheers. Even the *Sun* complimented him, "San Diegans have a right to lift their hat to John D. Spreckels."

Back in 1902 the old San Diego & Eastern Railroad Company, incorporated in 1871, was revived with George W. Marston as President. Between 1902 and 1906, $42,000 was raised by San Diegans. They were hopeful this company could raise enough funds to build a railroad from San

137

Diego to the Colorado river. Then Spreckels came out with his announcement. He promptly bought out the San Diego & Eastern and paid back to subscribers every cent they had put up. Needless to say, the subscribers were not only delighted, they were amazed, and gave Spreckels their enthusiastic support. Spreckels said he wanted no subsidies from any person or government. He wanted to do it himself, to be independent. Actually, it was later learned that Spreckels had received assurances of support from Harriman and the Southern Pacific. But most of the cost was borne by Spreckels personally. The railroad had come to mind during his illness. By his illness, and the San Francisco earthquake, San Diego gained a railroad.

In January, 1907, the survey began for the railroad, to go through National City, the Carrizo Gorge and through forty-four miles of Baja California. One million dollars was paid for rights-of-way as far as Jacumba. Spreckels personally went to Mexico City to obtain the right-of-way through Mexico. A silver spike was driven at the foot of Twenty-Seventh Street on Admission Day, 1907, marking the start of construction. John F. Forward, Jr., Mayor, turned the first sod. Present as honored guests were both A.E. Horton and Frank Kimball, who must have looked on with satisfaction, knowing that at last their dream was coming true. However, it would be twelve years before the railroad was completed. It proved far more expensive than expected and there were many setbacks and disappointments. The cost of building twenty-one tunnels through Carrizo Gorge was tremendous. World War I came along, but because of the strategic need for this railroad, it was allowed to continue and obtain materials denied others. Finally the great day arrived. On November 15, 1919, a group of dignitaries joined Spreckels in his personal railway car and rode to a spot east of Jacumba where a golden spike was driven in, commemorating the completion of the San Diego, Arizona & Eastern Railroad. December 1 to 6 were days of celebration in San Diego and Imperial. It was called "Transcontinental Week." December 1 was John D. Spreckels Day in San Diego. There was a long parade downtown that ended at the Organ pavilion, where a program honoring Spreckels was held. Credit for the completion of the railroad was given to the persistence and tenacity of Spreckels. It was the railroad that finally created the close tie between San Diego and Imperial. The two communities had been so near and yet so far, where travel back and forth was concerned.

The total cost of the railroad was said to be eighteen million dollars. It saved 100 miles to the East—important then, but so insignificant today!

The population in 1906 had grown to 35,000, more than double that of 1900, and this was before Spreckels' announcement of a new railroad. Residents were too cautious to call it a boom, but businessmen were confident prosperity was just around the corner. Then came the earthquake on April 18 that demolished San Francisco and left the rest of California in a state of shock. San Diegans rallied to the support of their friendly neighbor to the north and sent $25,000 worth of food, clothing, tents, stoves, and other necessities, to aid the sufferers. John D. Spreckels was not the only refugee from San Francisco to make his way to San Diego. Others, not so prominent, also came south to see what San Diego had to offer, and many stayed.

In May, 1906, groundbreaking was held for the new Elks' Building at the corner of Second and D, now the site of the Crocker National Bank Building. Father Horton was present and asked to turn the first shovelful of dirt. Horton was a charter member of the Elks when it was organized in 1890 and was always vitally interested in its work. Horton had never smoked, and very much disliked the smell of cigar smoke. Nevertheless, in his later years he had to get used to it, because of his membership in several Lodges, and having to attend meetings in smoke filled rooms.

In a school bond election that year, $120,000 was voted for new schools. The city schools now had on their payroll 100 teachers, whose salaries ranged from $900 to $1200 a year for high school teachers, and $600 to $800 for teachers in the grammar schools. In all, there were 4,243 children enrolled. That was the year the old Russ High School burned to the ground (some said with a little assistance). With the insurance money and some of the funds from the school bonds, a beautiful new Grey Castle was built on Russ Hill. The mammoth stadium was added in time for the exposition of 1915.

The town was expanding north and east. In January, 1906, there was only one building in Normal Heights. By the end of the year, there were forty. In that year the Southern California Mountain Water Company built the University Heights Reservoir and began furnishing water to that area from its Otay reservoir.

The announcement of plans for the railroad caused another spurt in business activity. William E. Smythe, the San Diego historian, referred to

1906: "An old epoch had closed; a new epoch had dawned."

Also in 1906, John H. Gay, owner of the Lakeside Inn, opened a racetrack in Lakeside. It was there, in April, 1907, that the racecar driver Barney Oldfield, in his machine the "Green Dragon," set his world speed record of sixty-five miles per hour.

In the same month that Barney Oldfield was setting a speed record in Lakeside, Father Horton was talking to a group of school children at the Public Library. In pouring out his heart to them, he said:

"I hope that the school children who are listening to me this afternoon will learn the lesson of San Diego thoroughly for themselves; that they will open their young hearts and receive the conviction in a few hours that it has taken the world of grown folks half a century to get beaten into their thick skulls—and that is that San Diego, California, has the finest harbor in the entire world; that the situation as a port is unrivalled, and that within the next 30 years it will be recognized as the best and largest port on the Pacific Coast, with a population of over a million souls."

Fig. 114 Horton breaks ground for the new Elk's Club, 1906

The city still does not quite have the million souls Horton prophesied. But childen, as well as adults, do agree that San Diego does have the finest harbor in the world.

One of the biggest events to occur in the city's history was the visit in 1908 of the Great White Fleet. It was President Theodore Roosevelt's idea to send a battle fleet to circle the globe to impress the world, and particularly Japan, that the United States intended to defend its interests in the Pacific as well as in the Atlantic. The Great White Fleet, under the command of Rear Admiral R.D. Evans, left the East Coast on December 16, 1907 and arrived in San Diego on April 14, 1908 for a four day stay. Sixteen battleships, seven destroyers and four auxiliary ships made a for-

Fig. 115 D.C. Collier

the red lights. On April 15 San Diegans came from far and near to crowd along D to watch another parade, probably never matched again in numbers. Five thousand crewmen marched up D accompanied by Navy brass and civic dignitaries, as well as military and local bands. So friendly were San Diegans and so impressive was the entertainment during their short stay that many officers and men who saw San Diego for the first time on that occasion returned later to make their home here. When the Great White Fleet sailed away all agreed it had "given San Diego a place in history."

While Spreckels was extending his street railway to the new subdivisions, Normal Heights, Hillcrest, and East San Diego, maintaining that "transportation determines the flow of population," D.C. Collier was busy promoting a railroad to Point Loma and Ocean Beach. In 1909 the population of Ocean Beach was only 100. The growth of this resort community had been impeded because of the lack of transportation. Collier and his Ralston Realty Company (later the D.C. Collier Company), purchased the tract north of the original Ocean Beach subdivision laid out by Carlson and Higgins during the boom years. Collier's purchase was bounded by Brighton on the south, Froude on the east, and the ocean and bay on the west and north. He then incorporated the Point Loma Electric Railroad for the purpose of providing the necessary transportation to his new development in Ocean Beach. This line went out Barnett to Voltaire and then west to the ocean. It meandered around Ocean Beach before returning on Voltaire, so it became known as The Loop Line. Local dignitaries received an engraved invitation to be guests of Collier on the first run of the railroad, which left from in front of the Union Building at 2:00 p.m. on Friday, April 30, 1909. This line was of short duration. Collier, like Carlson, was ahead of his time, so far as the beach area was concerned. Collier Park and Collier Junior High School in Ocean Beach are on land donated to the city by this dedicated man who is entitled to be remembered as one of San Diego's great City Builders. Collier was reputed to have owned the first automobile in San Diego. It was a small three-wheeler, of French design, allegedly capable of doing twenty-five miles an hour, and would go fifty miles on three quarts of gasoline. After his first attempt to drive the little machine, the Union reported: "Mr. Collier has perfect control over his machine and can make it go wherever he wills." However, Collier soon became disgusted with it. It had to be towed so regularly he finally gave it away.

midable and impressive sight as they lay at anchor off Point Loma. Nothing so momentous had happened in San Diego before. Mayor John F. Forward, Jr. and other dignitaries were on hand to greet Admiral Evans and the other officers and men. Sixteen thousand sailors, with four months' pay in their pockets, swarmed over the city. A stand was set up in the plaza, furnishing free lemonade. Drinks were not free in the bars, but lunch and snacks were. The whole town was gaily decorated with flags and bunting. Residents invited the men to their homes for dinner, and the Stingaree District had out the red carpet as well as

With the advent of the automobile, street and road improvements became a necessity. In 1907, $75,000 in bonds for street improvements were voted, the first real road improvements since the early nineties. This was followed in 1909 with a $1,250,000 bond issue. The city then appointed three Road Commissioners, John D. Spreckels, A.G. Spalding and E.W. Scripps. It was a strange combination, these three S's, two of whom were bitter antagonists. Under their direction, roads were constructed around the Coronado Strand (Spreckels' influence), to Point Loma (Spalding's influence), and in the back country (Scripps' influence). They were all dirt roads and did not hold up for too long. Spalding, who made his residence at the Theosophical Headquarters, was one of the subdividers of Loma Portal. He had long complained that Point Loma, which has "the finest view in the world," was completely inaccessible. He used his own money, as well as the government's, to open up the road out Point Loma to the lighthouse.

Another important event in the history of San Diego's early development was the decision by the Chamber of Commerce to bring John Nolen, an architect and city planner, to San Diego. He was asked to make a study of the city and then submit his recommendations. In 1909 his plan was submitted to the public. He suggested that public buildings should be grouped together around a central plaza, and that the block bounded by Front, First, C, and

Fig. 116 Proposed Palm Room for the U.S. Grant Hotel

Fig. 117 Louis J. Wilde

these more conservative years he was a City Builder, a businessman and banker, but promoter he was for sure. He did not have much money of his own, but he was always able to get and use other people's money.

Within a few years after his arrival, he had organized four new banks, the Citizens Savings Bank, the American National Bank, and the United States National Bank, all in San Diego, and the First National Bank of Escondido. He was the first President of each, and so must certainly hold the record of being president of more banks in San Diego than any other man.

He built the beautiful Louis J. Wilde Building, occupied by the United States National Bank on the northeast corner of Second and D. In 1909 he built the ten story American National Bank Building, at the northeast corner of Fifth and D, then the tallest building in town. The American National Bank merged with the First National Bank in 1917 when Spreckels assumed control of both banks. This building then became the First National Bank Building.

In 1904 Wilde built the Pickwick Theatre, just north of D on Fourth, across from the Horton House. It also housed some offices, on the ground floor. The name Wilde was prominently marked on the facade of this attractive new theatre, which featured vaudeville and stock companies and later became a motion picture theatre. One of the tenants in the building was J.T. Hayes, who ran a jitney bus service from San Diego to El Centro over the route of the old "Jackass Trail." He used the curb in front of the theatre as a depot. When the service was expanded, it took the name of Pickwick Stages, the forerunner of the Greyhound Bus Company.

In 1907 Wilde purchased the mansion on the northeast corner of Twenty-Fourth and D at the top of Golden Hill, with a magnificent view of the city and down D Street, which at his suggestion and under his urging became Broadway in 1914. He wanted to be known as "the man who made Broadway." Even with the competition of Spreckels, Wilde did all right on his Broadway. However, before the name could be changed, the name Broadway had to be removed from a street in Mission Hills, which was renamed Montecito Way. Wilde agreed with Spreckels that San Diego politicians were trying to keep the town an old people's home. He wanted to get action—to get the city in motion, and bent every effort to do just that.

In 1908 when the U.S. Grant Hotel fell into financial difficulties and stood uncompleted and boarded

D, be designated a public plaza. Around this block would be grouped the Courthouse, City Hall, Post Office and an Opera House. At that time, the Courthouse was the only building of any importance surrounding the suggested plaza. At the foot of D, Nolen suggested a large Bay Plaza. Commercial interests should be confined south of E, while pleasure and business should be north of E. He also set up a plan for a park system. Nothing was done with Nolen's plan, in spite of much talk. It was resurrected and revised in 1926 when the plan for a City Mall was presented to the voters. It is still, however, on occasion referred to by city planners.

And while Spreckels was buying up property and building on the south side of D, Louis J. Wilde was working the other side of the street. Wilde arrived here in 1903. Had he come in the eighties, he would have been described as a promoter, but in up, an eyesore on San Diego's main street, Wilde, through his banking connections, was able to raise the money to complete the building and he became part owner with U.S. Grant, Jr. The new and luxurious hotel, containing 437 rooms, was completed at a cost of over one million dollars. Its formal opening was on October 15, 1910. To celebrate the opening of the hotel, Wilde presented to the city a Grecian fountain for the plaza. He commissioned Irving J. Gill, one of San Diego's most noted architects, to design the fountain. It was to be lighted by electricity, something new and spectacular. Both day and night water effects would be beautiful. In the daytime, the colored effect would be obtained by water flowing over a dome of prismatic glass which reflected all colors of the rainbow. As the water fell over the dome, it broke into spray and mist. At night, hundreds of incandescent globes were used to secure fifteen different color effects. The cost of the fountain was over $10,000. The dedication ceremony for the fountain was on the evening of the hotel opening. A large crowd was on hand to see the fountain turned on for the first time. The crowd gasped with delight and amazement, and enthusiastic cheers went up for Wilde and Gill. Incorporated in the fountain were three portraits: Juan Rodríquez Cabrillo, Junípero Serra and Alonzo E.

Fig. 118 U.S. National Bank, Second and D (Broadway)

Horton. Then, as now these men were the acknowledged founders of San Diego. Wilde went on to become Mayor in 1917, after a tempestuous campaign against George W. Marston, dubbed Geraniums vs. Smokestacks campaign. He served two terms and then left San Diego for greener pastures, but not without having left his mark on the history of the town, and on the street he named Broadway.

There was another change in the city government in 1906 when a new City Charter went into effect. The City Council then was reduced from twenty-seven to nine, but not without strenuous objection from Spreckels who maintained that twenty-seven men would be harder to corrupt than nine. The new charter also provided for the Initiative, Referendum and Recall, one of the first for any city in California. Elections were still on a partisan basis.

Every election brought forth a so-called "Clean-Up" campaign, referring to the Stingaree District.

Fig. 120 Irving J. Gill

Fig. 119 Plaza Fountain

The district now was bounded by Sixth, H and the bay. Dozens of cribs lined the streets, particularly on Fourth. Saloons provided rooms upstairs, with entry through the rear door marked with a red light. There were also some fine "Parlor Houses." The Green Light, at Third and I, was a two-story building built around a courtyard, with a balcony. Rooms with kitchenette were rented to girls who preferred individual enterprise. San Diego's most famous Madam was Ida Bailey, owner of Canary Cottage, on the west side of Fourth between H and I. She and her girls went only first class. Every day they would parade through town in a fine carriage rented from the Diamond Carriage Company. The driver frequently stopped at a flower shop on Fourth Street to buy fresh posies for the girls to carry.

In 1909 a powerful triumvirate came into power affecting the Stingaree, Judge George Puterbaugh, Justice of the Peace (1909-14), Walter Bellon, Sanitary Inspector, and Keno Wilson, Chief of

Police (1909-17). Wilson expressed himself as opposed to closing down the red light district, saying he preferred to have it where the police could keep an eye on things. Finally the hue and cry became too much, citizens wanted to get their city cleaned up before the coming exposition. And so, on November 10, 1912, San Diego's most noteworthy "raid" took place. In a mass arrest, 138 women were rounded up and jailed. They probably were expecting it, for they put up no resistance. The police claimed they had closed all the bawdy houses in San Diego, including the Oasis, at the foot of Fourth, and The Turf, at Fourth and J, two of the more notorious. The next morning all 138 were lined up in front of Judge Puterbaugh, who fined each $100.00 and then suspended the fine on the condition they got out of town "forthwith" and did not return. They all trooped down to the Santa Fe Station and bought passage to Los Angeles. It was noted, however, quite a few bought round trip tickets.

After a "cooling off" period, it was noticed that some of the "girls" were back in town. They slipped in quietly, but instead of returning to their old haunts, rented large homes in the new residential districts and in Mission Hills. The Madams now were "hostesses." There was even a chain of houses started in East San Diego on El Cajon Boulevard, then just a dirt road on the way to La Mesa. This is not quite what San Diegans had in mind, but the 1912 raid had the desired effect of at least closing up once and for all the Stingaree District, which was now just a memory.

The first suggestion that San Diego should have an exposition was made in 1909. San Francisco then announced plans for a Panama Pacific Exposition in 1915, celebrating the completion of the Panama Canal. San Diegans reasoned that their city was to be the first port in the United States from the Canal and that it too should honor the occasion. Furthermore, it might produce the shot in the arm the city needed to spur business, again in the doldrums.

G. Aubrey Davidson, then President of the Chamber of Commerce, is credited with the original idea, and again it would be the Chamber of Commerce that would lead the way to its implementation. Davidson suggested "something unusual was needed to attract people to San Diego." Perhaps an exposition was the answer. In 1910 over one million dollars was raised by public subscription and a one million dollar bond issue was voted by the city, whose total population was less than 40,000, for the newly incorporated

Panama-California Exposition Company. Colonel D.C. Collier was appointed Director General for the exposition. Collier became known as "the creative genius of the 1915 Exposition." He contributed $500,000 of his own money toward the park development. It was his idea that the architecture should be in keeping with San Diego's Spanish heritage. The construction of the Indian Village was also his idea. He made many trips to South America and to Washington, D.C., in the planning and promotion of the exposition. San Diego's Congressman William Kettner also was of great help in matters needing government assistance. Collier went on to become Director General of the Philadelphia Sesquicentennial Exposition, and the Century of Progress Exposition in Chicago. He returned to San Diego in 1932 where he died November 14, 1934, at the age of sixty-three. He was easily recognized by the five gallon hat and Windsor tie which he always wore. His title "Colonel" was an honorary one, but was appropriate.

Fig. 121 Officer Gonzales and Chief of Police Wilson

Fig. 122   The residence of Charles S.
Hamilton, corner of
Seventh and Beech

John C. Olmstead was employed as landscape designer. He and many of the members of the old Chamber of Commerce Park Development Committee wanted the buildings to be grouped at the southwest corner of the park. Collier and the members of the City Park Commission thought otherwise. They wanted the buildings in the center of the park, and their decision was final. Olmstead was so unhappy he resigned. The Park Commissioners then employed Bertram Grosvenor Goodhue of New York, considered the greatest authority on Spanish architecture in the United States, to design buildings using the Spanish Colonial type of architecture. Carleton M. Winslow was his assistant. Many of the buildings were replicas of famous landmarks in Spain and Mexico.

Frank P. Allen, Jr., Director of Works, was the designer of the bridge that was named for the discoverer of San Diego, Juan Rodríquez Cabrillo. The exposition would be known as The Garden Fair. In 1909 the park still had no name, so the Park Commissioners conducted a contest to give it a name. Many names were suggested, including Cabrillo, Balboa, Coronado, Horton and Spreckels, but the honor went to Balboa, discoverer of the

146

Pacific. On November 1, 1910, City Park became officially Balboa Park.

Ground breaking for the fair was on July 19, 1911. A three day celebration was held to mark the great event. This was one city project that received almost unanimous support. No expense would be spared to make it a success. The plans were eagerly watched and the results approved enthusiastically.

The fair opened at midnight, December 31, 1914. President Wilson pushed a button in Washington officially opening the Panama California Exposition in Balboa Park. Governor Hiram Johnson was present for the dedication of the California Tower, the state building. John D. Spreckels and his brother, Adolph B. Spreckels, donated to the city the fabulous Spreckels Organ Pavilion, then the largest outdoor organ in the world, at a cost of $125,000. In addition, John D. Spreckels had given $100,000 in cash when the exposition was first proposed, and then gave another $100,000 for the second year. At the dedication of the organ on the night of December 31, 1914, sixty thousand persons were in attendance. Samuel Shortridge, later United States Senator from California, was the speaker. John F. Forward, Jr., then President of the Park Commissioners, accepted the organ on behalf of the city. For years Spreckels paid all the expense of maintaining the organ, and employed Dr. Humphrey J. Stewart as official organist, who gave free concerts every day of the year.

In the first year of the exposition, there were three million visitors to San Diego, most of whom came only to see the fair that was being so widely publicized, described as being breathtakingly beautiful. No one was disappointed. It was a fairyland, something to be seen only in a beautiful dream, but miraculously, it was real. When the fair closed at the end of 1916, it was with a financial balance. The exposition did much to advertise San Diego. Its name and reputation of being a garden spot became known throughout the United States and even the world. Many foreign visitors arrived, usually after having been to San Francisco, and then told they should not miss San Diego's little gem of a garden fair.

The exposition also helped to put San Diego on the map as a military base. Franklin D. Roosevelt, then Assistant Secretary of the Navy, accompanied his superior, Josephus Daniels to San Diego. They were much impressed with its possibilities as a naval base. Soon North Island was purchased, a destroyer base established, and then the Naval Hospital. Some Marines were stationed on Dutch Flats, the beginning of the Marine Base. It was apparent now that because of its geographic location the government would have to maintain San Diego as a military base for the protection of the border and the West Coast. San Diego, from a place of no importance, was at last becoming recognized.

The beginning of the new century also saw the end of an era. The early settlers who had stuck with the town through good times and bad were now passing away. Matthew Sherman, the first resident of Horton's new town, a civic leader and a former mayor, died in 1898. In 1906 Horton lost his devoted friend, E.W. Morse, who died on January 17. Morse, although quiet and unassuming, was just as energetic as Horton and as intent on building San Diego into a great city. His career began as a merchant and Wells Fargo agent in Old Town, and in New Town he was a banker, civic leader and builder of one of the finest business blocks, the Pierce-Morse Building at the northwest corner of Sixth and F. In his quiet way he made numerous cultural donations, including a valuable lot for the Society of Natural History, and his part in the setting aside of City Park should never be forgotten. Just the year before his death, on January 4, 1905, the Chamber of Commerce had honored both Alonzo E. Horton and E.W. Morse, Charter Members, by making them Honorary Life Members of that organization. Upon Morse's death, Horton said, "There is no man that has been truer to the interests of San Diego than E.W. Morse."

The beloved Father Ubach, native of Spain, but for over forty years a faithful pastor in San Diego, died March 26, 1907. His funeral was one of the largest ever held in San Diego. St. Joseph's Cathedral was packed to capacity. Thousands stood outside in respect. Indians arrived carrying wildflowers they knew he loved. He was laid to rest in Calvary Cemetery in Mission Hills where an impressive memorial was erected over his grave.

Horton's long life was now coming to a close. Fortunately, until his last illness, his health was good and his mind keen. He moved more slowly, but his eyes were still clear and blue, his complexion pink, and his beard long and white. He was a familiar figure in his frock coat and silk top hat driving about each day in his one-horse carriage, tipping his hat to acquaintances or stopping to chat with a friend. He always kept a sharp eye on new improvements being made in his city.

O.W. Cotton, another great city builder, and developer of Pacific Beach and East San Diego has said, "Horton, in the early 1900's, used to drop by my real estate office to reminisce about old times. It was depression times, but Father Horton was still just as optimistic as to the future of the city as he had been in 1885."

Occasionally Horton would stop in Ingersoll's, a candy and ice cream store on Fifth between E and F, for a dish of ice cream, or he would ask for "a Sarsaparilla, please." Whatever he wanted, it was on the house. He also would be seen stopping at the "Coffee Club," a "Poor Man's" cafe where coffee, soup, pie and doughnuts were sold for five cents apiece. He would go in, perch on a stool and order milk and pie. In this cafe, patronized more by newcomers striving to make ends meet, he was not always recognized and sometimes no one spoke to him. But he shared with the strangers a common bond—the need to conserve money. After the $100 a month payments from the city for the plaza ceased in 1903, his means were meager. Occasionally friends helped out, but unobtrusively, as Horton was proud and sensitive. One can understand the Hortons' financial condition a little better when it is known that Mrs. Horton, then nearing sixty, sought employment, something unusual in those days, especially for one with her social position. In 1904 she became Librarian at the State Normal School, at a salary of seventy-five dollars per month. This partly made up for the loss of the $100 from the city. She continued on after Horton's death, retiring in 1910.

Horton had once been the wealthiest individual in southern California, the most influential in his city and one of the most powerful political figures in the county. He had given away land now valued in the millions, but he never considered himself a philanthropist. He had made and lost fortunes, but he was never bitter or discouraged. He was now virtually penniless, but never was he a pathetic figure, he was too vital for that. To the last, he was San Diego's most important salesman. He radiated enthusiasm and cheer wherever he went.

On his ninety-fifth birthday, October 24, 1908, Horton was interviewed by a *Sun* reporter on the veranda of his State Street home overlooking the bay and city. He was quoted as saying: "It is the most beautiful place in the world to me, and I had rather have the affection and friendly greetings of the people of San Diego than all the rulers of the world."

Shortly before Christmas, Horton fell ill, and about a week before his death was taken to Agnew Sanitarium at Fifth and Beech. On January 7, 1909, at 11:00 a.m., he passed away quietly in his sleep. His physician, Dr. James A. Jackson, said,

"The end was very peaceful. He died with a serene smile on his face." The doctor, in an interview with a reporter, was quoted thus:

"His last thoughts when conscious were for San Diego. He talked of nothing else. He did not seem to realize at any time that he was near death. He confidently expected to live to see San Diego a great city and repeatedly told of his hopes. I remember about the last talk of any length that came from his lips. He asked to be taken to the roof garden of the sanitarium. We did so. He looked out over the city which he had founded and pointed at the various old landmarks and the evidences of growth, proudly at the latter. He said he hoped to live to see San Diego a city of 100,000."

Funeral services were held on Saturday, January 9, at two o'clock, in Elks' Hall, Second and D. The Masonic services were open to the public. Before the services, eight thousand men, women and children streamed past his flower covered casket to pay their last sad respects. The *San Diego Union* reported: "Rich and poor, high and low alike, join in doing honor to this venerable man. Never more fitting was the phrase 'lying in state'. All through the hours set apart for this last farewell look, a constant stream of men, women and children streamed past to bid him goodbye."

An editorial in the *Union* on January 8, said:

The entire community will mourn the death of Alonzo E. Horton. His passing comes as a distinct personal loss to almost every resident of San Diego. No citizen is so well known to so large a number of people as was the venerable "Father" of San Diego. For it was his pleasure, especially during recent years, to go frequently among the people of the city that owes so much to him. He delighted to mingle alike with old and young, rich and poor, residents and strangers, and to all he endeared himself by his cordial friendliness. . . The grand services which he rendered to the city whose growth received from him its first impetus are known to all. It is probably not exaggeration to say that no other man ever did so much to create a city where there was not even the nucleus for one as did "Father" Horton in the case of San Diego. It was directly through his personal efforts that San Diego occupies its present advantageous site. Forty years ago he built deeply and well for the city that was to come . . . For all time the names of the three men will be inseparably joined to the history of San Diego, Cabrillo, discoverer, Serra, pioneer of Christian civilization whose memory is revered by all, and Horton, the founder whose foresight made possible the San Diego of today.

But aside from all that he did for the city that was so dear to his heart, Alonzo E. Horton will be mourned as the man and citizen, upright, kind and courteous, honored and esteemed in larger measure than falls to the lot of many men.

At the funeral services, John B. Osborne, in an elo-

quent eulogy, said, "He was a plain, typical American western pioneer, with a true vision and optimism infinite." Lolita Levet Rowan, who had been like a daughter to Horton, sang in her lovely contralto voice some of his favorite songs.

After the services, his body was borne through the streets to its last resting place in Mount Hope Cemetery. The streets were lined with people, the men bareheaded, the women touched with emotion, and the children subdued. Saturday afternoon business stopped, stores and offices closed, as all who could crowded the streets to watch the impressive funeral procession, led by mounted policemen. They were seeing the end of an era, and of this, many were aware.

By coincidence, William Heath Davis, who always considered himself the founder of San Diego, because of his effort to establish a city in New Town, also died in 1909, in Hayward, California at the age of eighty-seven. Davis' effort to establish a city, even though unsuccessful, is noteworthy and must not be forgotten. Neither should the memories of all those other pioneers who deserve the title "City Builder," and whose names are all too frequently forgotten except in the annals of historical journals.

After Horton's death, his widow stayed on in the home on State Street for a short while and then sold it in April, 1910. Horton left no estate subject to probate. On December 11, 1897, he had conveyed to Lydia M. Horton the lots in Middletown on which their home was situated. After describing these lots, the only known land still remaining in his name, the deed went on to state, "together with all other real property in the City of San Diego belonging to me, or in which I may have any interest." This deed was not recorded until a few days after Horton's death. It was on the basis of this deed that the county later paid to Horton's heirs an amount, alleged to be $25,000, for a quitclaim deed to the courthouse site in order to close out, once and for all, any reversionary interest they might have had.

In an interview, Mrs. Horton said of her husband, "He had a great broad vision. He foresaw all that came to pass in San Diego in his lifetime. He was never surprised at any of the great improvements which were made here in his later years. One might think that he would have been sorry when the old Horton House, the fine hotel that he built, was torn down to make room for a modern structure, but he was not sorry—to the contrary, he was glad to see the fine new building go up."

Horton's niece, Grace Bowers, said of him, "My uncle lived little in the past. He lived in robust health until he was 95. He was an energetic Connecticut Yankee, driven by one purpose, building a city."

Even before Horton's death, civic leaders commissioned the noted British sculptor, Allen Hutchinson, to create a bust of Horton to present to the city. A plaster model was made from life and exhibited at the Bank of Commerce. Six hundred dollars was subscribed to have the bust cast in bronze, but sufficient funds were not forthcoming and the project was dropped. The life sized plaster bust, an excellent likeness, was found a few years ago in storage at the San Diego Historical Society's Serra Museum.

In 1913 the Order of Panama took up the call for a suitable monument to Horton. Subscriptions of $1.00 per person were solicited. This effort also fell short of accomplishment.

In April, 1937, at a meeting of the San Diego Historical Society at the Cafe Del Rey Moro in Balboa Park, George W. Marston was the speaker. He spoke of Horton, and said San Diego had never properly recognized Horton, but his fame would increase with the years and suggested a monument of some sort be erected to his memory. Marston also referred to the three men who will go down in history as the founders of San Diego: Cabrillo, Serra and Horton.

Again, on September 9, 1938, at an Admission Day luncheon in the U.S. Grant Hotel, George W. Marston, then San Diego's "Number One Citizen," was the guest speaker. This time he proposed that a suitable marker, in memory of Horton, be placed at the new Civic Center on the waterfront. He credited the city's remarkable growth to the optimism and "never say die" spirit of Father Horton, which he had instilled in the early residents.

Finally, in August, 1939, Edgar Hastings, on behalf of the San Diego Historical Society, announced the Society would furnish as a gift to the city a bronze plaque costing $500. It would be erected in the central corridor of the Civic Center.

The plaque was dedicated on September 30, 1940. It reads as follows.

MEMORIAL
TO
ALONZO E. HORTON
1813-1909
FOUNDER OF THE MODERN
CITY OF SAN DIEGO
1867
FIRST IN CIVIC VISION
FIRST IN HEROIC ADVENTURE
FIRST IN COURAGE AND DETERMINATION
HERE HE FOUNDED THE CITY OF HIS DREAMS
THEREFORE WE CALL HIM
FATHER HORTON

George W. Marston, in dedicatory remarks, said:

"On Mr. Horton's birthday, the 24th of October, 1870, it was my good fortune to become a hotel clerk in the new and wonderful Horton House facing the Plaza, where the Grant Hotel is now. It has therefore been a personal and particular pleasure for me to take a part in providing the memorial that is being dedicated today.

"As two generations have now passed in the life of the city, the historical perspective clearly reveals that Alonzo Erastus Horton was the real founder of the modern City of San Diego. Our local historian, W.E. Smythe, well says that 'His title to this distinction is as clear as that of Cabrillo to the discovery of the bay, or that of Serra to the founding of the mission'. So we may feel well assured that the man we honor today is truly worthy of this community expression, and this building, a splendid symbol of the founder's dreams, is a fitting home of our tribute to his memory . . . It is idle to speculate as to when and how a new San Diego would have been started if Mr. Horton had not undertaken the job. But it is safe to say that we wouldn't be here today to talk about it . . . Since Mr. Horton's death in 1909, the new generation knoweth not their first citizen. They may say, 'We recognize him as a pioneer founder, but we want to know what kind of a man he was.' Read Smythe's History of San Diego. I endorse Mr. Smythe's opinion that Alonzo Horton was a man of principle, just and honest in his dealings with the new community, and forwarding their welfare as well as his own. I myself knew him for nearly forty years, and can testify to his temperate life, his kindness to neighbors and his boundless generosity to public needs . . .

"Mr. Horton's place as founder of the City of San Diego is assured for all time. History will add his name to the roll of the notable pioneers of California. Here in San Diego we feel not only proud of his wide fame, but also the affection that is indicated in the last words of our memorial: 'Here he founded the city of his dreams, therefore we call him Father Horton.' "

The plaque and a large portrait of Horton were hung on the city's side of the Civic Center Building, in Middletown. When the city administra-

Fig. 125   Bust of Alonzo Horton by Allen Hutchinson

tion moved into the new Community Concourse, leaving the old Civic Center Building to the County, no one thought to move the memorial into the new quarters, in Horton's Addition, an even more appropriate location.

Today, Horton's memory is recalled by Horton Plaza, not so designated officially by that name until 1925, and by Horton Elementary School at 5050 Guymon Street. There is a Horton Avenue, branching off from Laurel and going up on Horton Hill, but it is mostly in a gully. All the homes he lived in, except the old Davis' house on Eleventh Street, have fallen victim to the wreckers. But the greatest tribute to Horton today is the great metropolitan city he did not live to see, except in his dreams. We can imagine him today, if such were possible, view-

Fig. 126 San Diego, October 1907, looking north across the Middletown addition

ing his city for the first time after seventy years. Words spoken by him more than seventy years ago would be even more appropriate today: "I am not surprised at what has happened here in San Diego. I have seen it all—the tall buildings and great ships at anchor, taller buildings and greater ships than I had ever seen. I dreamed it all."

The city of his dreams has come true, and with it, he would be well pleased.

Bibliography

Adams, H. Austin. *The Man John D. Spreckels.* San Diego: Frye and Smith, 1924.

Black, Samuel F. *History of San Diego County.* Chicago: S.J. Clarke Publishing Company, 1913.

Brennan, John Edward. "History of Ocean Beach, 1542-1900." Unpublished Manuscript, San Diego State College, 1960.

Chase, Waldo. "Memoirs." San Diego Historical Society Library and Manuscripts Collection.

Cleveland, Daniel. "San Diego's Pueblo Lands." San Diego Historical Society Library and Manuscripts Collection.

Davis, Edward J.P. *Historical San Diego.* San Diego, 1953.

Davis, William Heath. *Sixty Years in California.* San Francisco: A.J. Leary, 1889.

Davis, William Heath. *Seventy-Five Years in California.* San Francisco: John Howell Books, 1967.

Donley, Ward T. "Alonzo E. Horton." Unpublished Masters Thesis, San Diego State College, 1952.

Dumke, Glenn S. *The Boom of the Eighties in Southern California.* San Marino: The Huntington Library, 1944.

Elliott, W.W. *History of San Diego County.* San Francisco: Elliott Publishers, 1883.

Gunn, Douglas. "San Diego, 1886." San Diego Historical Society Library and Manuscripts Collection.

Heilbron, Carl H., ed. *History of San Diego County.* San Diego Press Club, 1936.

Hensley, H.C. "Early San Diego." Vols. I, II, III. San Diego Historical Society Library and Manuscripts Collection.

Higgins, Shelley J. *This Fantastic City, San Diego.* City of San Diego, 1956.

Hopkins, H.C. *History of San Diego.* San Diego: City Printing Company, 1929.

Knox, Donna Marilyn. "Old Town vs. New Town, 1869-71." Unpublished Manuscript, San Diego State College, 1949.

MacPhail, Elizabeth C. "Allen Hutchinson, British Sculptor (1855-1929)" *The Journal of San Diego History,* XIX (Spring 1973), 21-38.

MacPhail, Elizabeth C. "The Davis House: New San Diego's Oldest and Most Historic Building." *The Journal of San Diego History,* XVII (Fall 1971), 31-38.

MacPhail, Elizabeth C. *Kate Sessions: Pioneer Horticulturist.* San Diego: San Diego Historical Society, 1976.

MacPhail, Elizabeth C. "San Diego's Chinese Mission." *The Journal of San Diego History,* XXIII (Spring 1977), 8-21.

MacPhail, Elizabeth C. "When the Red Lights Went Out in San Diego." *Brand Book Number Three.* San Diego: The San Diego Corral of the Westerners, 1973.

Marston, Mary Gilman. *George White Marston.* 2 Vols. Los Angeles: The Ward Richie Press, 1956.

McGrew, Clarence Alan, *City of San Diego and San Diego County.* Vols. I, II. Chicago: The American Historical Society, 1922.

Miller, Max. *Harbor of the Sun.* New York: Doubleday and Doran, 1940.

Nadeau, Remi. "City-Makers, The Story of Southern California's First Boom." San Diego Historical Society Library and Manuscripts Collection.

Phillips, Irene. *The Railroad Story of San Diego County.* National City: South Bay Press, 1956.

Pourade, Richard F. *The Glory Years.* San Diego: San Diego Union-Tribune Publishing Company, 1964.

Pourade, Richard F. *Gold in the Sun.* San Diego: San Diego Union-Tribune Publishing Company, 1965.

Rolle, Andrew F. "William Heath Davis and the Founding of American San Diego." San Diego: San Diego Union Title Insurance Company, 1952.

San Diego Historical Society. Biographical Files, Miscellaneous Books and Manuscripts.

San Diego Public Library. California Room, Miscellaneous Books, Documents and Manuscripts.

San Diego Union. Newspaper Files, San Diego Public Library.

Shepherd, Jesse Aland. "Diary, 1872." San Diego Historical Society Library and Manuscripts Collection.

Smith, Walter Gifford. *The Story of San Diego.* San Diego: City Printing Company, 1892.

Smythe, William E. *History of San Diego, 1542-1908.* Vols. I & II. San Diego: The History Company, 1908.

Stewart, Don M. *Frontier Port.* Los Angeles: The Ward Richie Press, 1965.

Wagner, Harr, Publisher. *Golden Era Magazine.* Miscellaneous issues.

Index